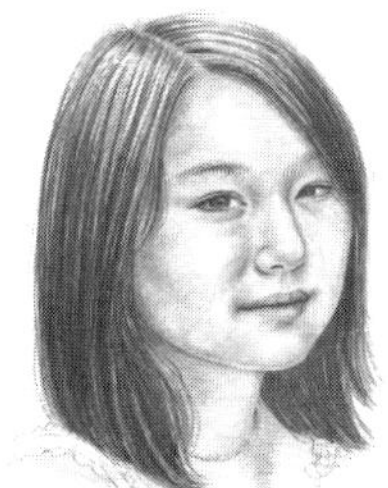

The Art of Drawing

FACES & FEATURES

Drawing faces is a challenge, but it's a challenge well worth taking on! From facial expressions and lighting to the unique characteristics that make us who we are, there are countless elements that make faces so exciting to draw. And with the billions of individuals in the world, you'll never run out of subject matter! But before you get started, you'll want to learn the simple techniques that can be employed to create realistic, beautiful portraits in pencil. In this book, you'll find not only plenty of helpful tips on tools and materials, shading, and other fundamental drawing techniques, but you'll also discover the information you need to re-create a range of faces—from varying ethnic traits to differing ages and hair styles. With a little practice, you'll be drawing all the distinct, unique individuals you please in no time! —*Debra Kauffman Yaun*

CONTENTS

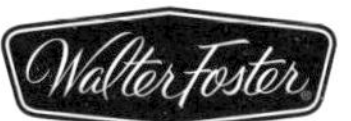

Selecting Tools and Materials

Graphite pencil is a versatile, practical medium that makes learning to draw convenient for any beginning artist. All you really need are a few basic tools, which are relatively inexpensive and easily can be taken with you almost anywhere. Even when you're just starting out, it's best to purchase the highest quality materials you can afford—better-quality materials last longer and will produce the most pleasing results. Here you'll find a quick overview of the items that I find most helpful. As you become comfortable with the basic tools and gain more drawing experience, you'll develop your own personal preferences.

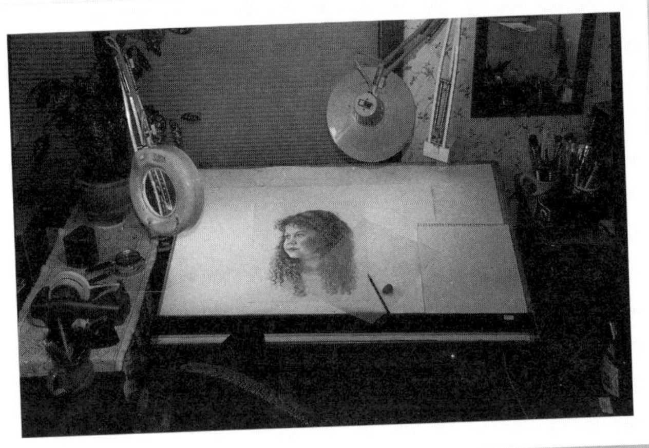

◄ **SETTING UP YOUR WORKSPACE** When choosing a place to work, comfort is key—you want to find a space that offers comfortable seating and good lighting so that you don't strain your back or your eyes! My work station, pictured at left, features an adjustable drawing table—allowing me to tilt my drawing surface—and a lamp that I can raise or lower as needed. All my tools are also within easy reach.

Choosing Pencils

The first thing you'll want to do when starting to draw is to purchase several different kinds of graphite pencils. Pencils are labeled with numbers and letters—and the combination of the two indicates the softness of the graphite. B pencils, for example, are soft and produce dark, heavy strokes, whereas H pencils are harder and create thin, light lines. An HB pencil is somewhere between the two, which makes it a good, versatile tool for beginners. The numbers that can accompany each letter indicate how hard or soft each pencil is—the higher the number, the more intense the softness or hardness of your lines will be. (A 4H pencil is harder than a 2H, and a 4B is softer than a 2B.) Practice drawing with each different kind of pencil and experience the variety of lines they can produce!

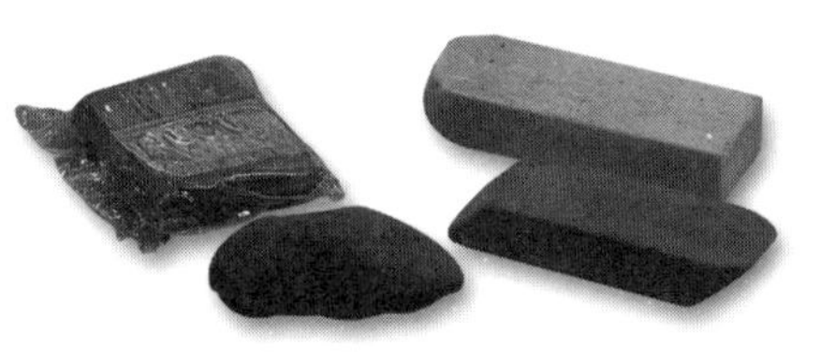

▲ **REMOVING TONE** You can use an eraser to make adjustments, correct mistakes, or pull out highlights in your portrait. Vinyl erasers are good to use for larger areas, whereas you can form the edge of a kneaded eraser into very small shapes to blend strokes for smooth transitions or to remove pencil from small areas. Just be sure you're gentle when erasing; scrubbing too hard can damage your paper or smudge your drawing.

▲ **SEEING THE WHOLE PICTURE** A magnifying glass is a helpful tool for artists, especially when using a photograph as a reference. Use a magnifying glass to enlarge any area of the photograph so you can see exactly what to reproduce. A reducing glass will make the image appear smaller so that you can better see any elements you may have missed. When using a photograph as a reference, hold the reducing glass above your drawing until it appears the same size of the photo. Then compare what you see through the reducing glass to the photo itself and make any necessary changes.

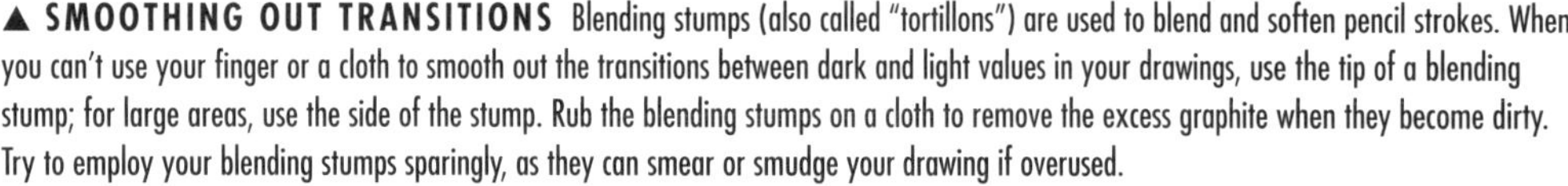

▲ **SMOOTHING OUT TRANSITIONS** Blending stumps (also called "tortillons") are used to blend and soften pencil strokes. When you can't use your finger or a cloth to smooth out the transitions between dark and light values in your drawings, use the tip of a blending stump; for large areas, use the side of the stump. Rub the blending stumps on a cloth to remove the excess graphite when they become dirty. Try to employ your blending stumps sparingly, as they can smear or smudge your drawing if overused.

▼ **FINDING A GOOD SURFACE** Drawing paper comes in a range of different surfaces, from smooth to rough; it also can be purchased in single sheets or in conveniently bound books. Most artists choose to use single sheets of high-quality drawing paper, but a sketch pad is often helpful for drawing on the go—especially when you're drawing faces and need to sit outside and people-watch for inspiration. You may want to begin drawing on paper that has a smooth- to medium-grain texture, as this kind of paper provides the most versatile drawing surface.

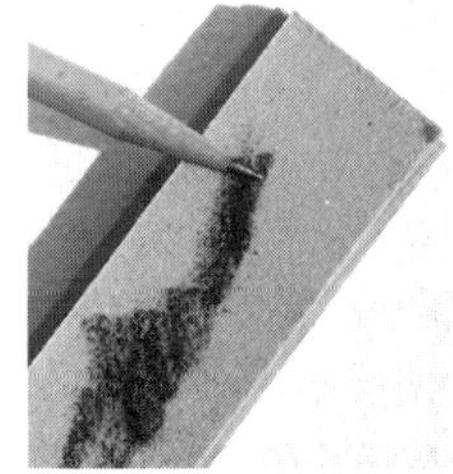

▲ **SHARPENING YOUR TOOLS** Electric sharpeners can quickly create a very sharp point on your pencil, but they aren't very portable. Smaller, handheld pencil sharpeners fit easily into a pocket or bag, and they allow greater control. A sandpaper block also can be used to form a variety of good pencil points.

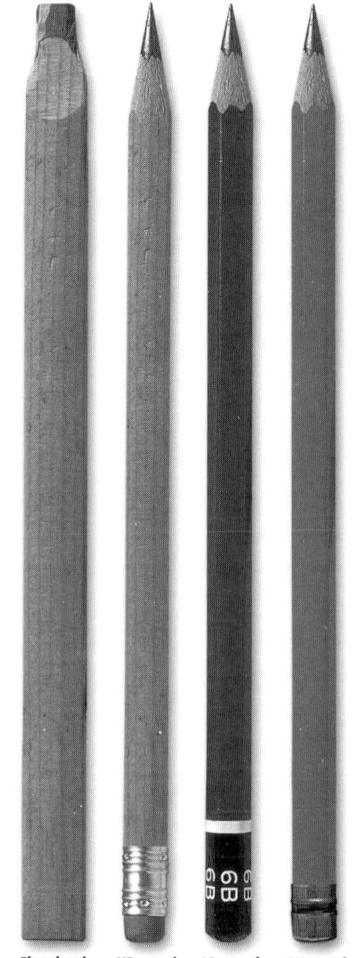

Flat sketch pencil   *HB pencil*   *6B pencil*   *2H pencil*

Mastering Shading Techniques

he key to transforming flat, simple shapes into convincing, lifelike forms is employing a variety of shading techniques. hade with soft strokes to create lighter tones, or put more pressure on your pencil and shade with heavy strokes to create darker tones. hese contrasts in *value* (the relative lightness or darkness of a color or of black) are what give depth and form to your drawings. Once ou've established the basic shape of your subject, try using the shading techniques shown below to apply dark and light values to your rawings—and watch your subjects come to life on paper!

REATING DEPTH

eparating the dark values of your shading from the light areas and ighlights of your drawing helps produce a sense of depth. When reating highlights, you can either "save" the white of the paper by aving areas of the paper white, or you can "retrieve" highlights by ulling out the value—removing graphite from the paper using the dge of a kneaded eraser that has been formed to a point.

PRACTICING BASIC TECHNIQUES

By studying the basic shading techniques below, you can learn to render everything from features to backgrounds. Shading in a side-to-side direction, with each stroke ending below the last, can create unwanted bands of tone throughout the shaded area. Instead, try shading evenly, in a back-and-forth motion over the same area, varying the spot where the pencil point changes direction.

EEING VALUES This value scale shows the gradation from black—the darkest value—through arious shades of gray, ending with white—the lightest value.

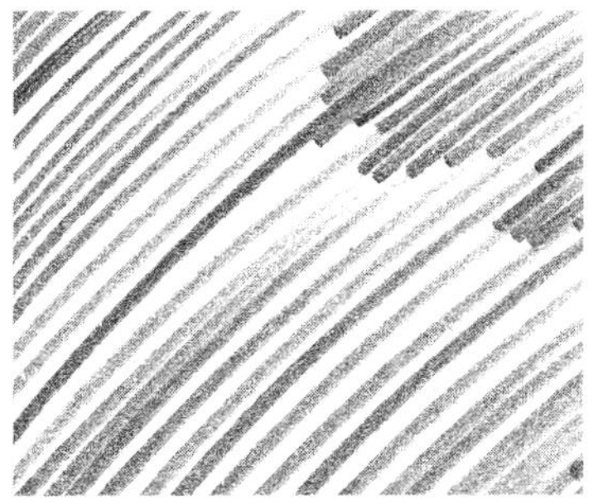

HATCHING Hatching is a shading technique in which you make a series of parallel strokes placed closely together.

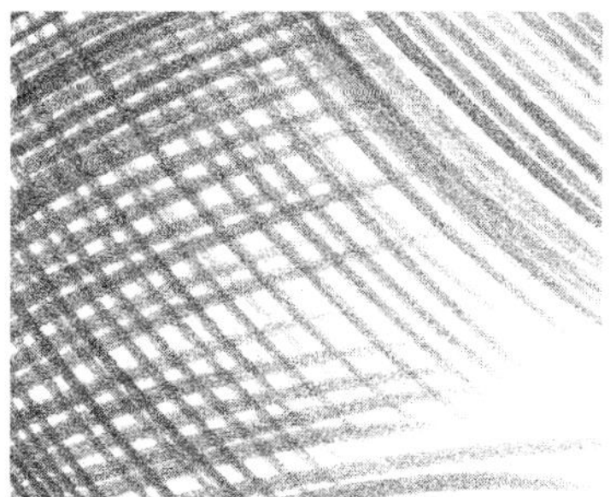

CROSSHATCHING Crosshatching is a shading technique in which you make a series of criss-crossed hatching strokes.

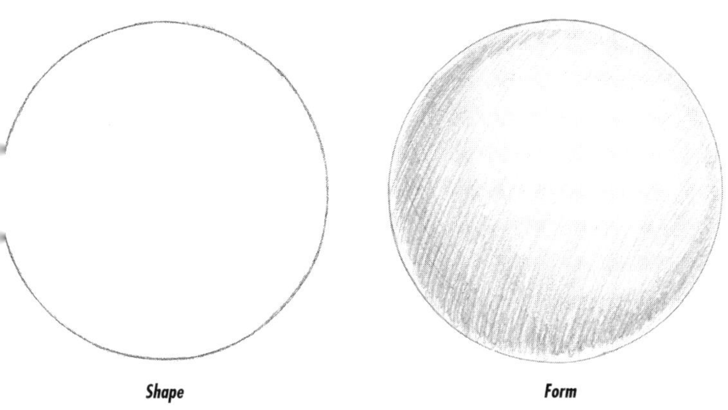

Shape   Form

HADING TO CREATE FORM When objects are viewed straight on, shading must be added create the illusion of depth. The plain circle to the left is simply a flat disk; but adding shading gives it rm, creating a three-dimensional sphere.

GRADATING To create graduated values (from dark to light), apply heavy pressure with the side of your pencil, gradually lightening the pressure as you stroke.

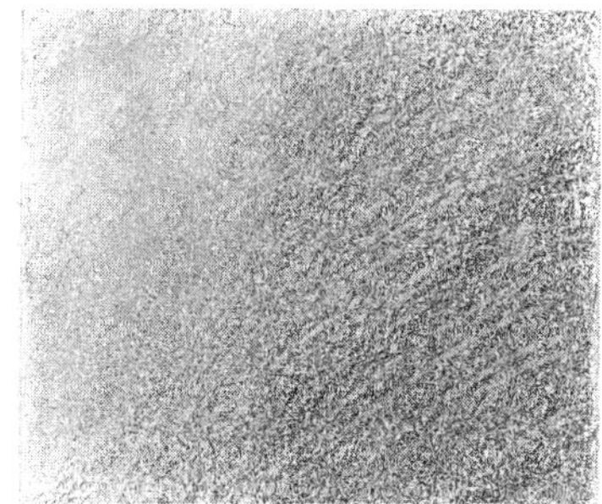

BLENDING To smooth out the transitions between strokes and create a dark, solid tone, gently rub the lines with a blending stump or a tissue.

Experimenting with Strokes

Learning to draw requires a certain amount of control and precision, so get used to the feel of a pencil in your hand and the kinds of strokes you can achieve. Before you begin sketching, experiment with different pencil grips to see how they affect the lines you produce. Fine detail work is more easily accomplished with a sharp pencil held as though you were writing, whereas shading is best done with the side of your pencil, holding it in an underhand position. Practice holding the pencil underhand, overhand, and in a writing position to see the different lines you can create.

You can also vary your strokes by experimenting with the sharpness or dullness of your pencil points. A sharp point is good for keeping your drawings detailed and refined; the harder the lead, the longer your pencil point remains sharp and clean. A flat point or chisel point is helpful for creating a wider stroke, which can quickly fill larger areas. Create a flat or chisel point by rubbing the sides of a pencil on a sandpaper block or even on a separate sheet of paper.

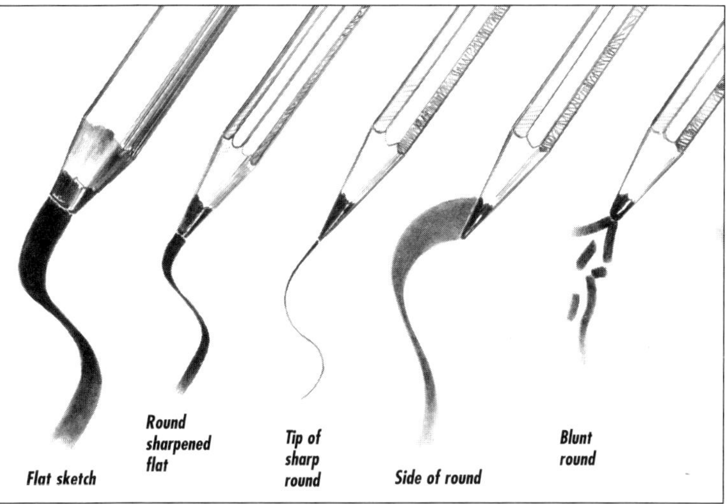

Understanding Anatomy

When drawing faces, it is important to be aware of the underlying structures of the head. Although the bones and muscles aren't visible in a final portrait, they provide the framework for the drawing, establishing the shape of the head and guiding the placement of the features. Having an understanding of the basic anatomy of the head will lend realism and credibility to your drawings.

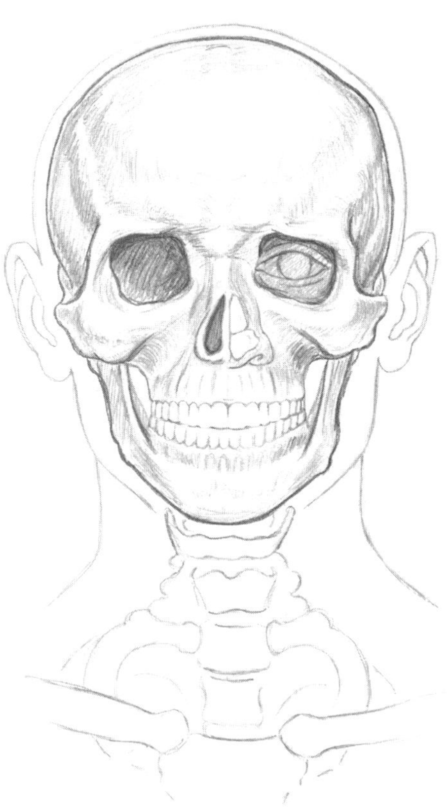

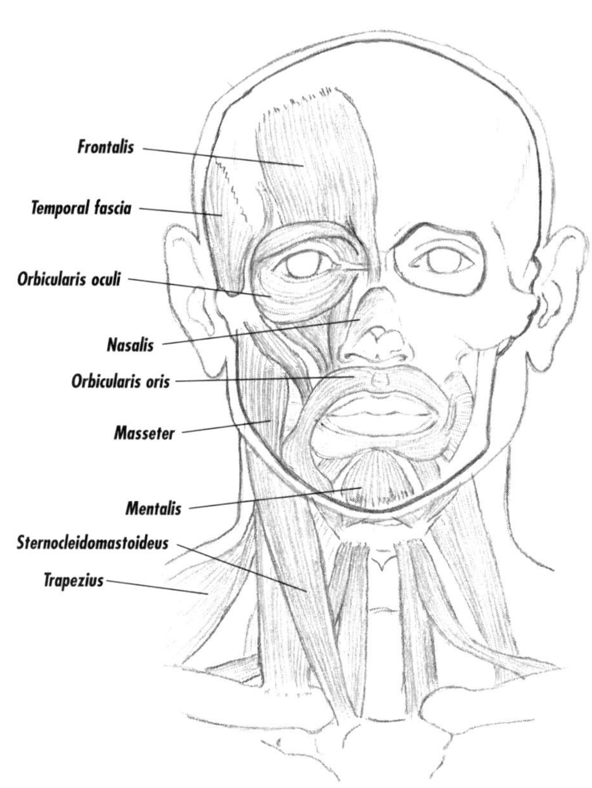

UNDERSTANDING BONE STRUCTURE   Becoming familiar with the bones of the skull and the way they affect the surface of the skin is essential for correctly placing the curvatures, ridges, and other prominent features of the head.

UNDERSTANDING MUSCLE STRUCTURE   When facial muscles contract, they affect the shape of the skin, cartilage, and underlying fatty tissues that cause the bulges, furrows, and other forms that create various facial expressions.

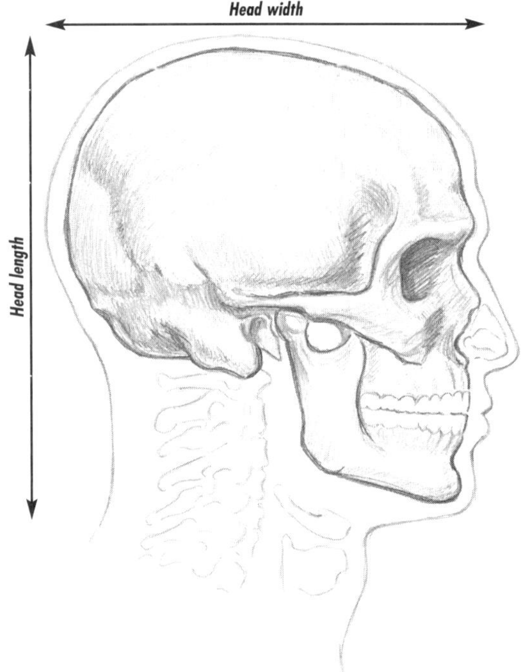

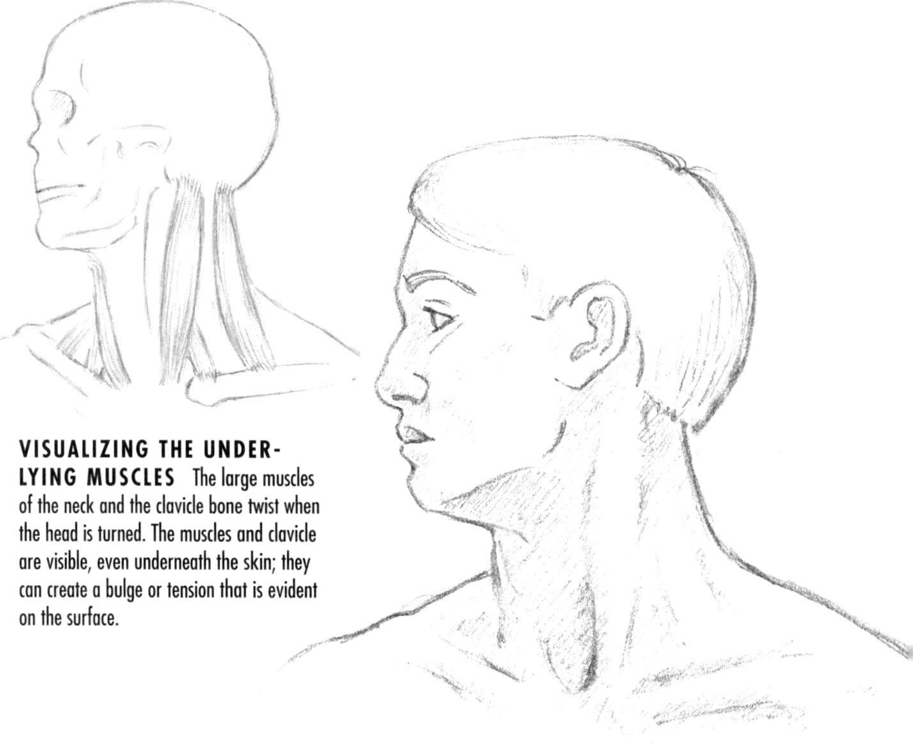

VISUALIZING THE UNDER-LYING MUSCLES   The large muscles of the neck and the clavicle bone twist when the head is turned. The muscles and clavicle are visible, even underneath the skin; they can create a bulge or tension that is evident on the surface.

SEEING THE SKULL IN PROFILE   In a profile view, it is easy to see how much area the back of the skull takes up. Notice that the length of the skull is just shy of its width.

Learning the Planes of the Face

Once you understand the basic structure of the head, you can simplify the complex shapes of the skull into geometric planes. These planes are the foundation for shading, as they act as a guide to help you properly place highlights and shadows.

The Effects of Light

▼ LIGHTING THE PLANES FROM ABOVE
When light comes from above, the more prominent planes of the face—such as the bridge of the nose and the cheekbones—are highlighted. The eyes, which recede slightly, are shadowed by the brow; the sides of the nose, bottom of the chin, and underside of the neck are also in shadow.

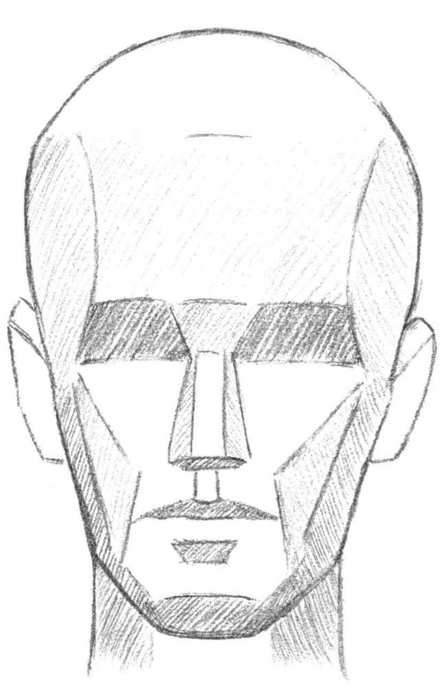

▼ LIGHTING THE PLANES FROM THE SIDE
Features are shaded differently when light hits the side of the face: The eyes are still in shadow, but the side of the face and neck are now highlighted.The shading on the head becomes darker as it recedes toward the neck; the sides of the cheeks appear "sunken"; and the ear casts a shadow on the back of the head.

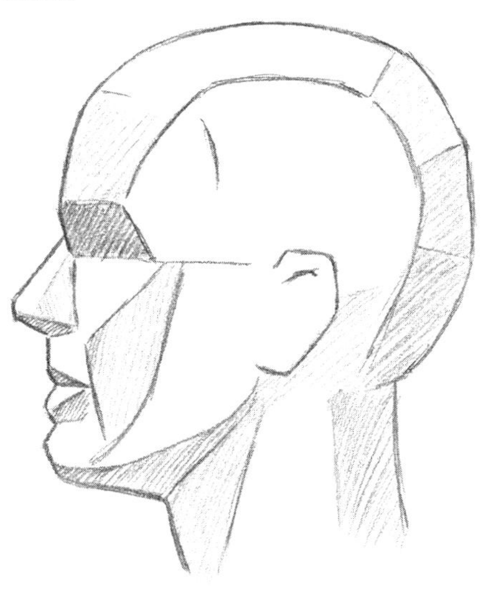

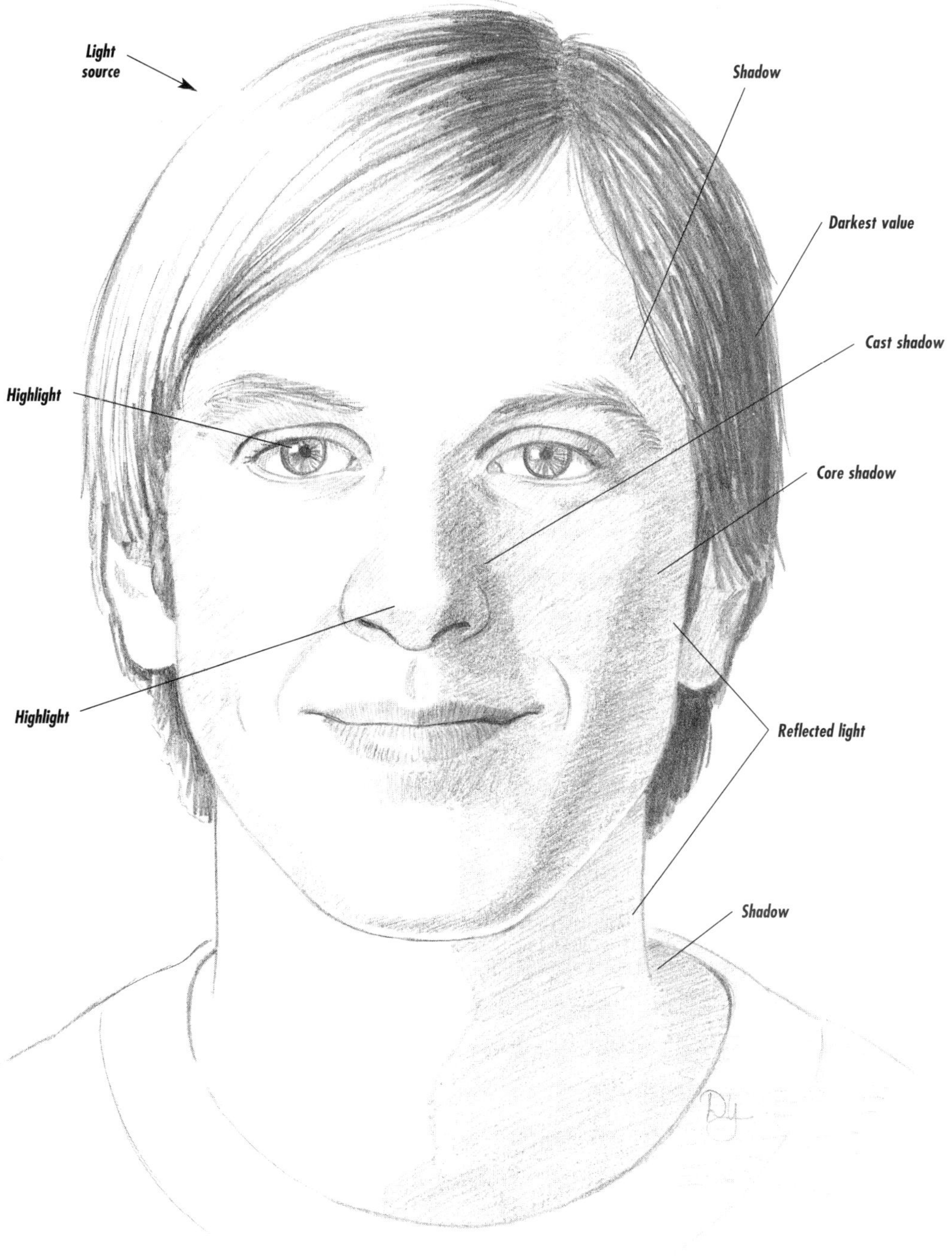

SHADING THE PLANES OF THE FACE   Many types and values of shadows contribute to the piecing together of all the planes of the face. *Core shadows*—or the main value of the shadows—are a result of both the underlying structure and the light source. Protruding objects, such as the nose, produce *cast shadows*, like the dark area on the left of this subject's nose. Highlights are most visible when directly in the light's path; here the light source is coming from above left, so the lightest planes of the face are the top of the head and the forehead. The darkest areas are directly opposite the light source, here the left side of the subject's face and neck. Even in shadow, however, there are areas of the planes that receive spots of reflected light, such as those shown here on the chin and under the eye.

Studying Adult Proportions

Understanding the basic rules of human proportions (meaning the comparative sizes and placement of parts to one another) is imperative for accurately drawing the human face. Understanding proper proportions will help you determine the correct size and placement of each facial feature, as well as how to modify them to fit the unique, individual characteristics of your subject.

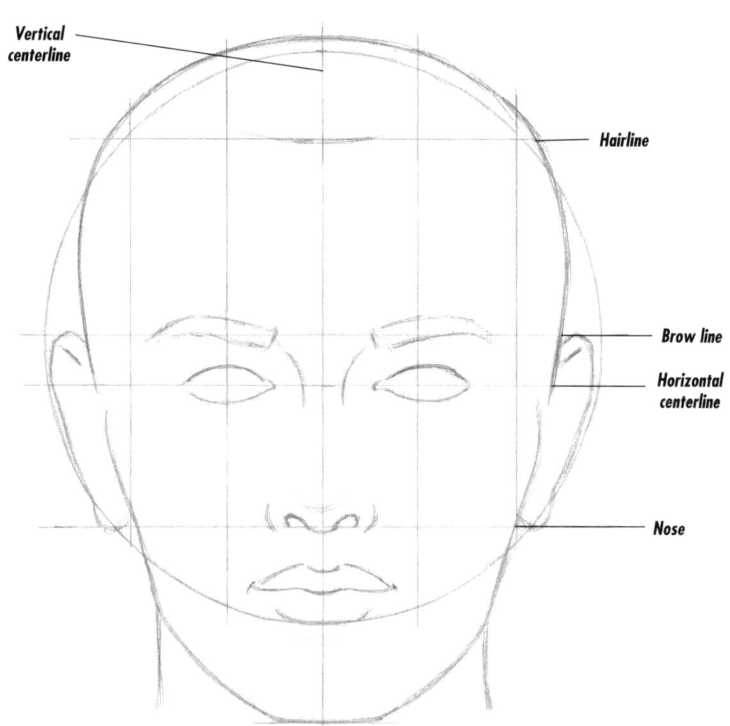

ESTABLISHING GUIDELINES   Visualize the head as a ball that has been flattened on the sides. The ball is divided in half horizontally and vertically, and the face is divided horizontally into three equal parts: the hairline, the brow line, and the line for the nose. Use these guidelines to determine the correct placement and spacing of adult facial features.

PLACING THE FEATURES   The eyes lie between the horizontal centerline and the brow line. The bottom of the nose is halfway between the brow line and the bottom of the chin. The bottom lip is halfway between the bottom of the nose and the chin, and the ears extend from the brow line to the bottom of the nose.

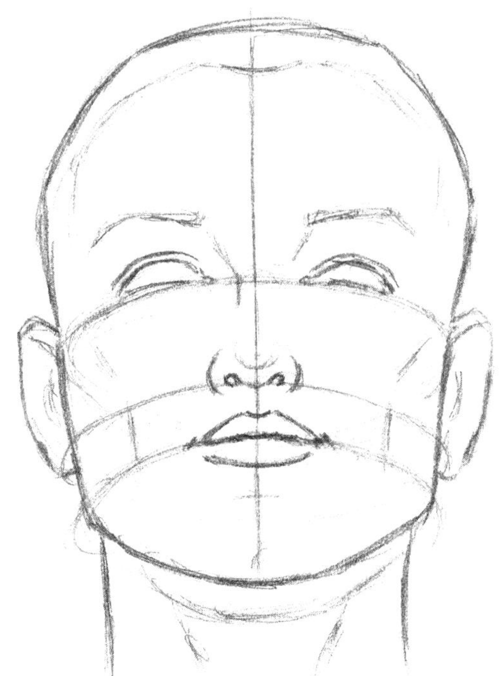

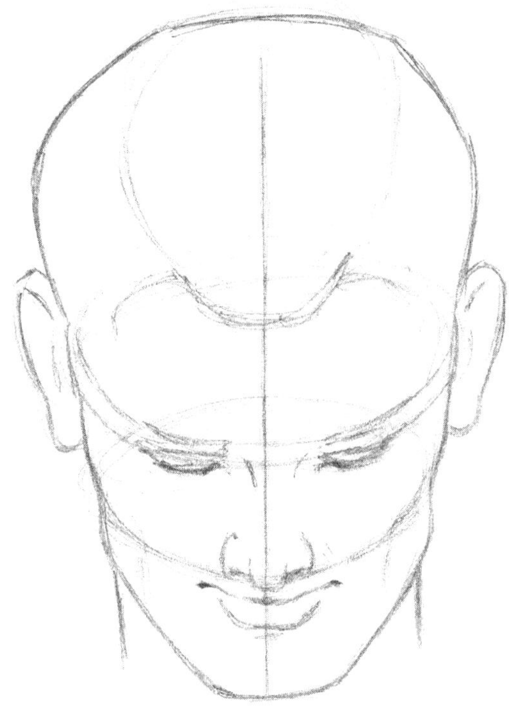

LOOKING UP   When the head is tilted back, the horizontal guidelines curve with the shape of the face. Note the way the features change when the head tilts back: The ears appear a little lower on the head, and more of the whites of the eyes are visible.

LOOKING DOWN   When the head is tilted forward, the eyes appear closed and much more of the top of the head is visible. The ears appear higher, almost lining up with the hairline and following the curve of the horizontal guideline.

Exploring Other Views

eginning artists often study profile views first, as this angle tends to simplify the drawing process. For example, in a profile ew, you don't have to worry about aligning symmetrical features. But the rules of proportion still apply when drawing profile views, as ell as the more complex three-quarter views.

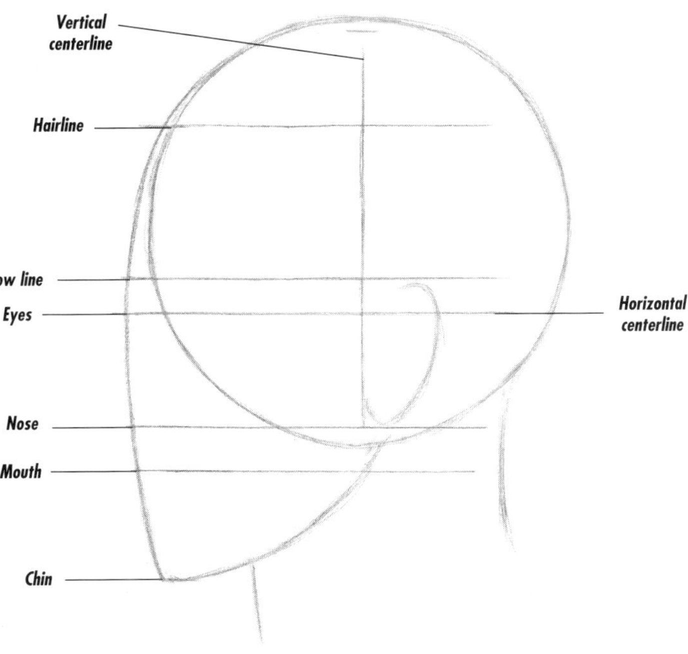

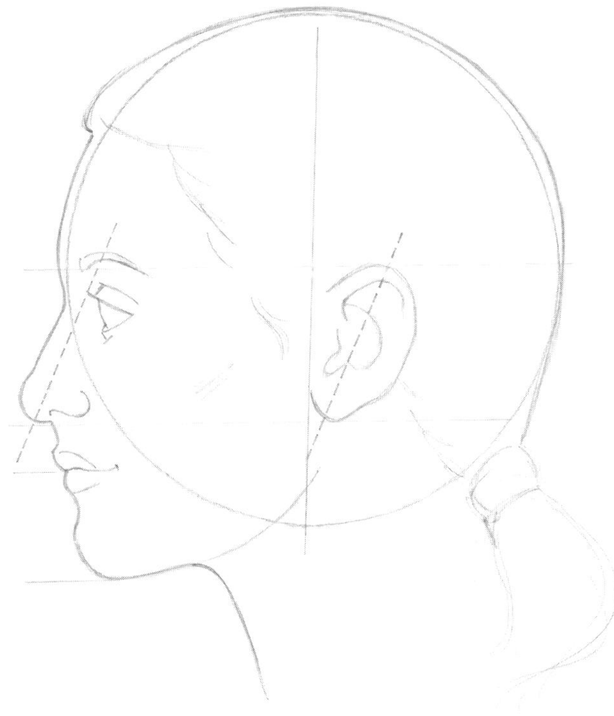

IMPLIFYING THE PROFILE To draw an adult head in profile, start by blocking in the anial mass with a large circle. Add two curved lines that meet at a point to establish the face and in. Place the ear just behind the vertical centerline.

PLACING THE FEATURES Use the large cranial circle as a guideline for placing the features. The nose, lips, and chin fall outside the circle, whereas the eyes and ear remain inside. The slanted, broken lines indicate the parallel slant of the nose and ear.

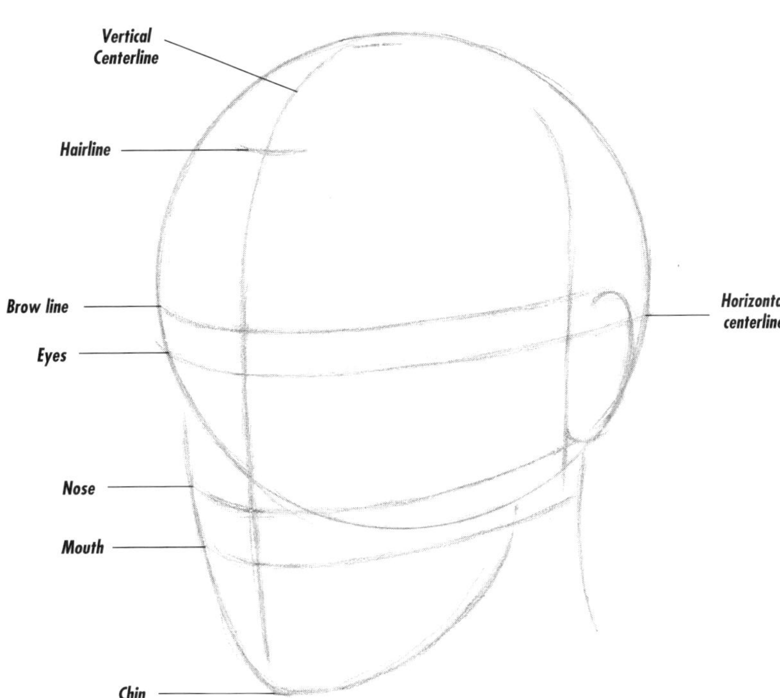

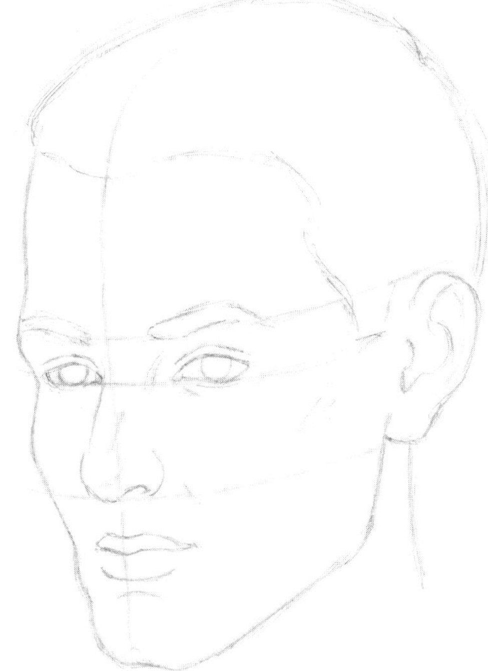

RAWING A THREE-QUARTER VIEW In a three-quarter view, the vertical centerline hifts into view. More of the left side of the subject's head is visible, but you still see only the left ear. s the head turns, the guidelines also curve, following the shape of the head.

DISTORTING THE FEATURES When the head turns, the eye closest to the viewer (in this case, the subject's left eye) appears larger than the other eye. This is a technique called "foreshortening," in which elements of a drawing are distorted to create the illusion of three-dimensional space; objects closer to the viewer appear larger than objects that are farther away.

Depicting Adult Features

If you're a beginner, it's a good idea to practice drawing all the facial features separately, working out any problems before attempting a complete portrait. Facial features work together to convey everything from mood and emotion to age. Pay attention to the areas around the features, as well; wrinkles, moles, and other similar characteristics help make your subject distinct.

EYES

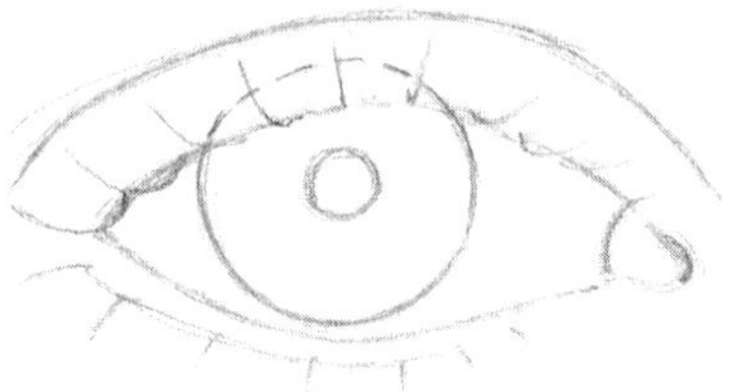

STEP 1   Make a circle for the iris first; then draw the eyelid over it. (Drawing an entire object before adding any overlapping elements is called "drawing through.") Note that part of the iris is always covered by the eyelid.

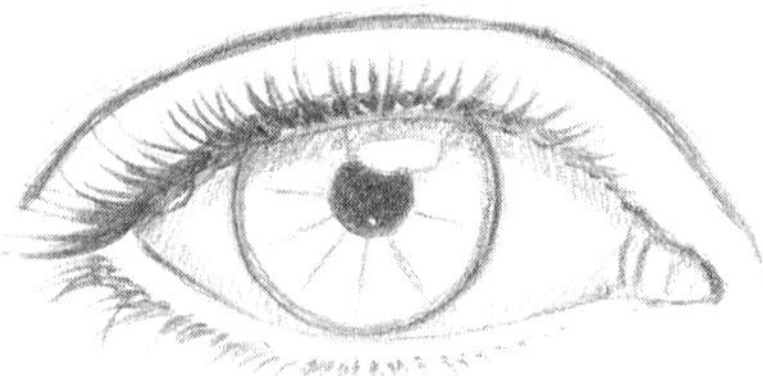

STEP 2   Start shading the iris, drawing lines that radiate out from the pupil. Then add the eyelashes and the shadow being cast on the eyeball from the upper lid and eyelashes, working around the highlight on the iris.

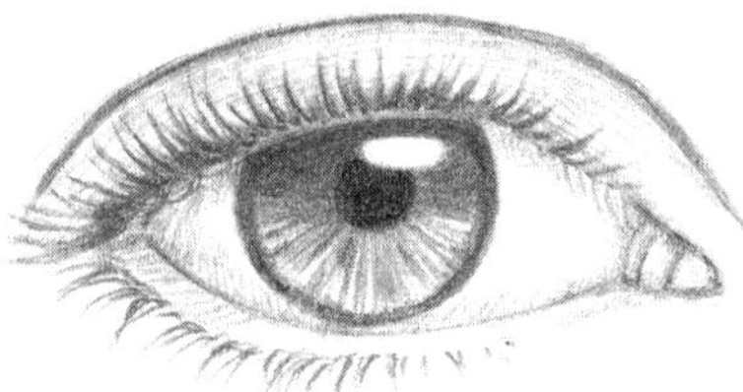

STEP 3   Continue shading the iris, stroking outward from the pupil. Then shade the eyelid and the white of the eye to add three-dimensional form.

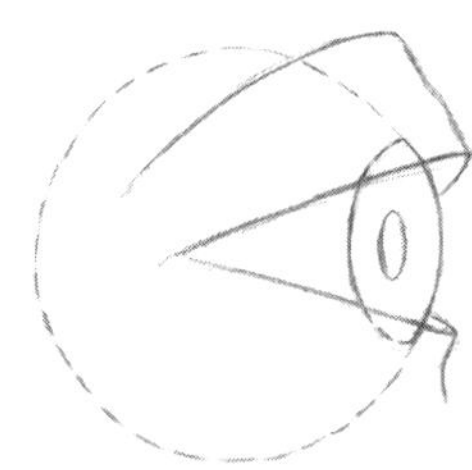

STEP 1   Draw through a circle for the eye first; then draw the eyelid around it, as shown. In a profile view, the iris and pupil are ellipses; the top and bottom of the iris are covered by the upper and lower eyelids.

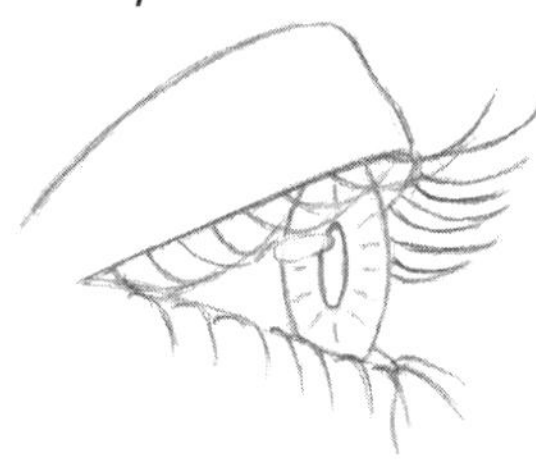

STEP 2   To draw eyelashes in profile, start at the outside corner of the eye and make quick, curved lines, always stroking in the direction of growth. The longest lashes are at the center of the eye.

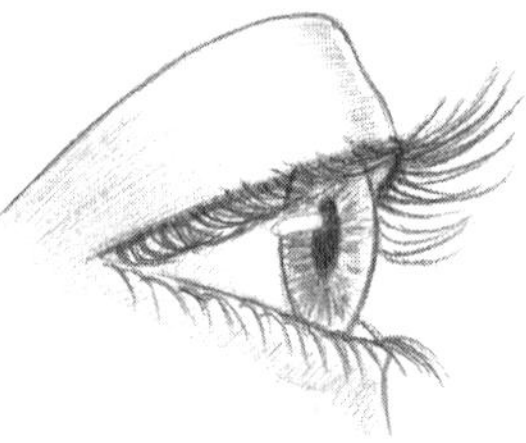

STEP 3   When shading the eyelid, make light lines that follow the curve of the eyelid. As with the frontal view, the shading in the iris radiates out from the pupil.

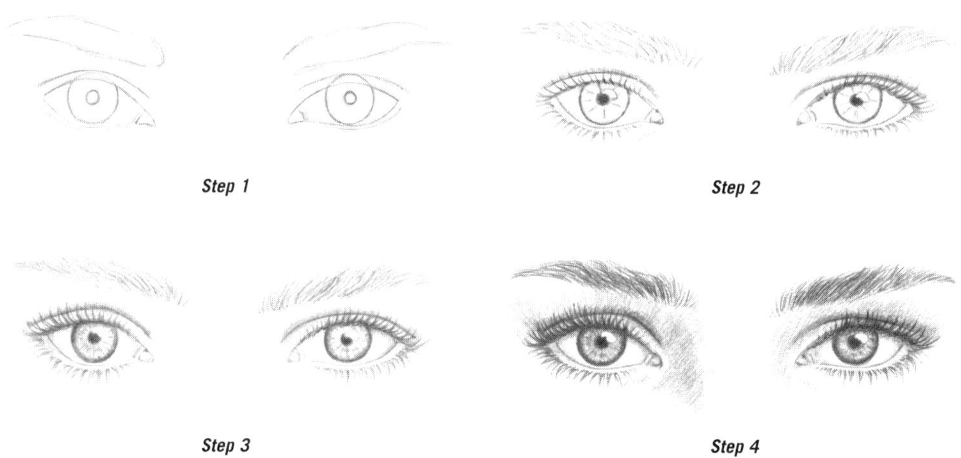

RENDERING A PAIR OF EYES   After becoming comfortable with drawing the eye itself, start developing the features around the eye, including the eyebrows and the nose. Be sure to space adult eyes about one eye-width apart from each other. And keep in mind that eyes are always glossy — the highlights help indicate this. It's best to shade around the highlights, but if you accidentally shade over the area, you can pull out the highlight with a kneaded eraser.

Varying Qualities

There are several characteristics that influence the final impression that a pair of eyes give: The shape of the eye, position of the eyebrows, length and thickness of the eyelashes, and number of creases and wrinkles can denote everything from age and gender to mood and ethnicity. Study the examples below to see how these different elements work together.

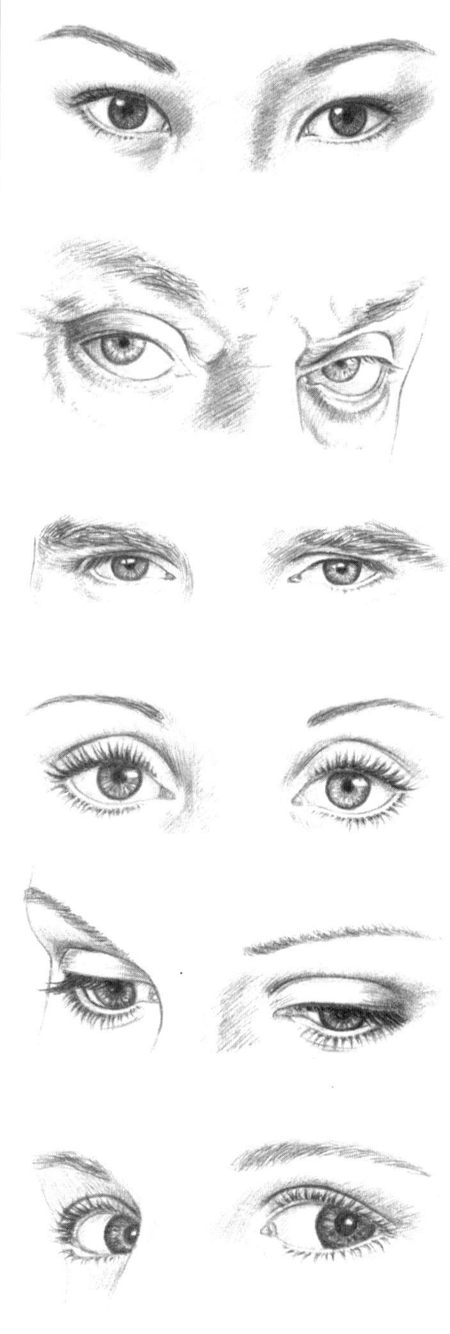

NOSES

RENDERING NOSES To draw a nose, I first block in the four planes—two for the bridge and two for the sides (see "Combining Features" below). Then I study the way each plane is lit before adding the dark and light values. The nostrils should be shaded lightly; if they're too dark, they'll draw attention away from the rest of the face. Generally men's nostrils are more angular, whereas women's are more gently curved.

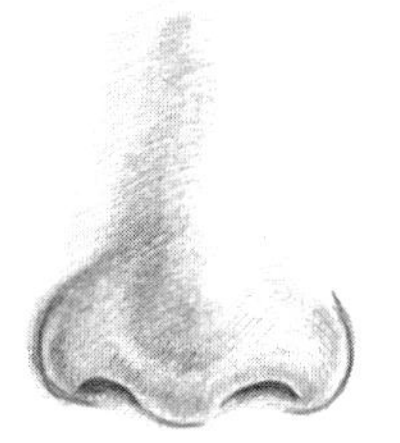

Round nose

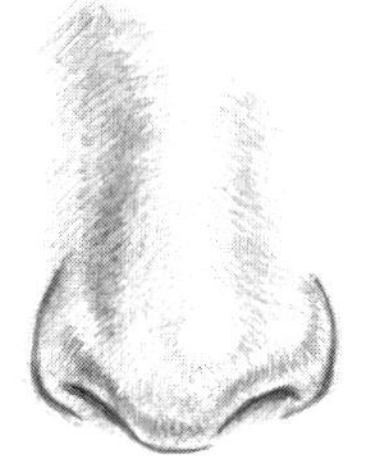

Flat nose

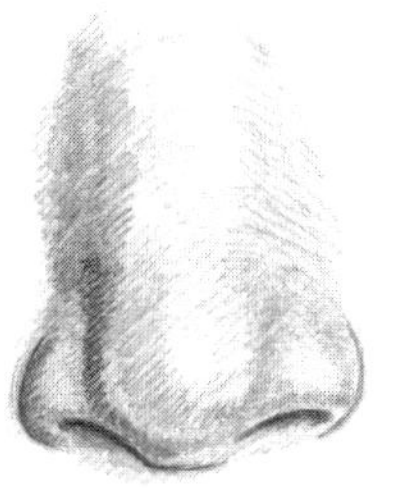

Bulbous nose

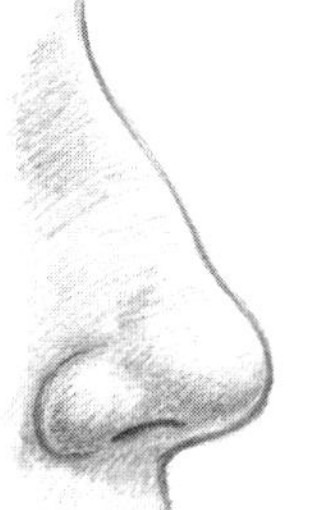

Ridged nose

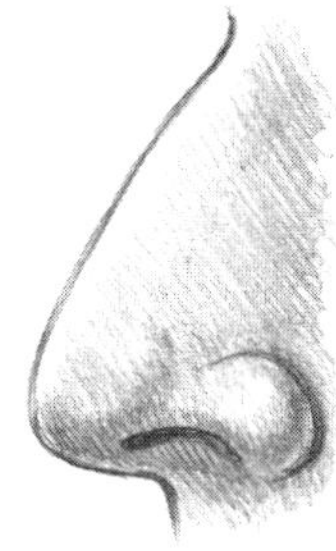

Hooked nose

EARS

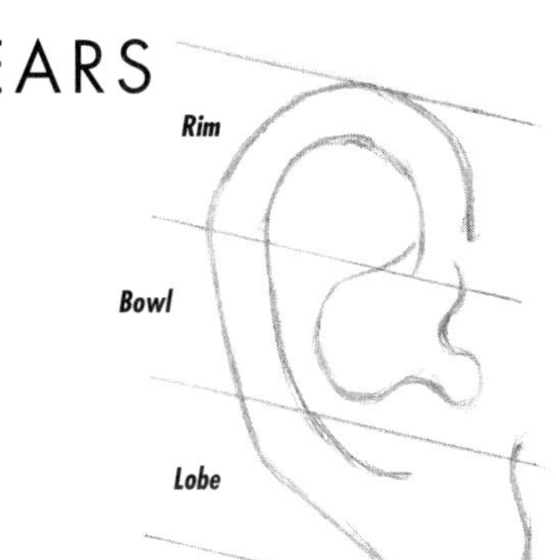

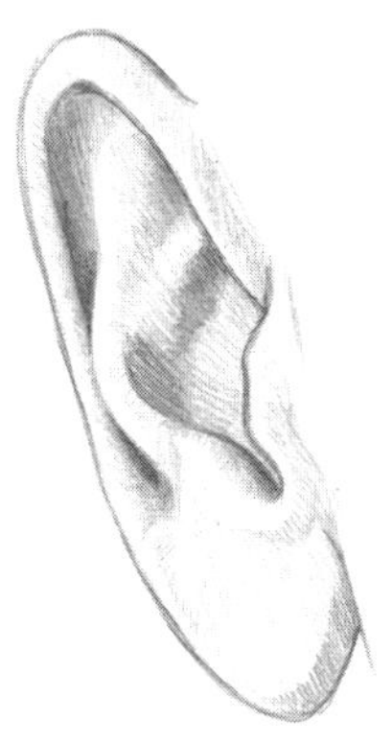

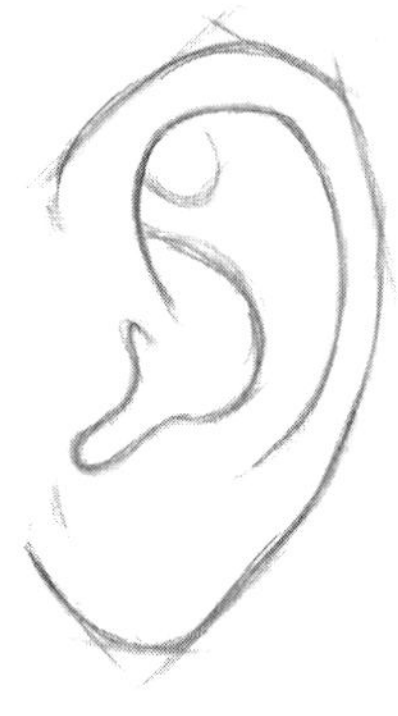

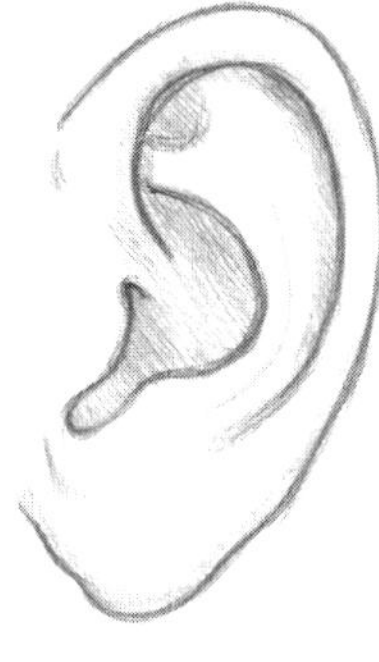

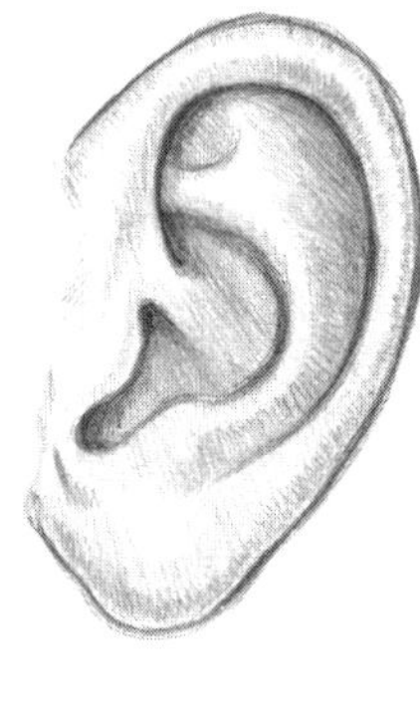

Step 1   *Step 2*   *Step 3*

DIVIDING THE EAR The ear is shaped like a disk that is divided into three parts: the rim, the bowl, and the lobe.

SIZING THE EAR The ear usually connects to the head at a slight angle; the width is generally about one-half of the length.

DEVELOPING THE EAR IN PROFILE I first block in the general shape, visually dividing it into its three parts. Next I start shading the darkest areas, defining the ridges and folds. Then I shade the entire ear, leaving highlights in key areas to create the illusion of form.

LIPS

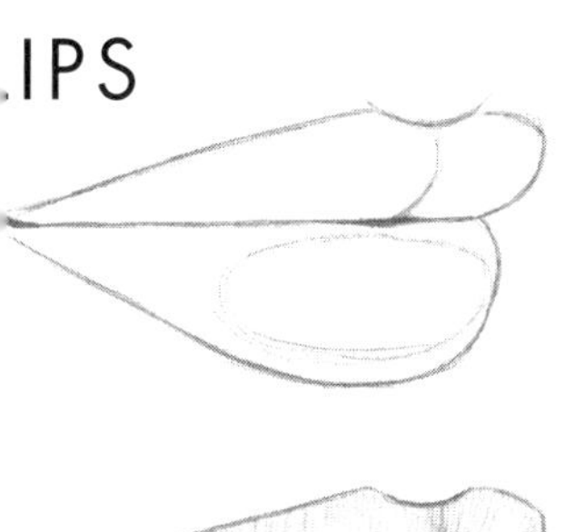

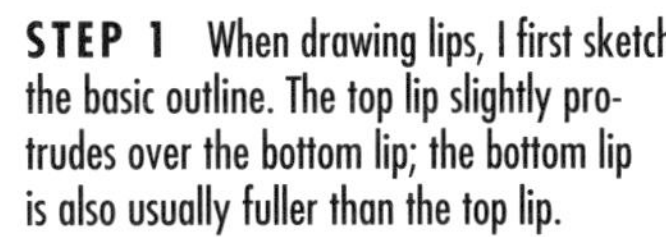

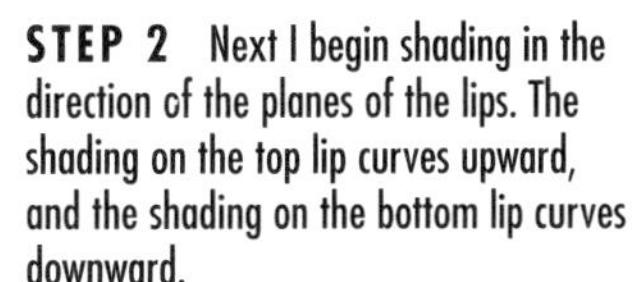

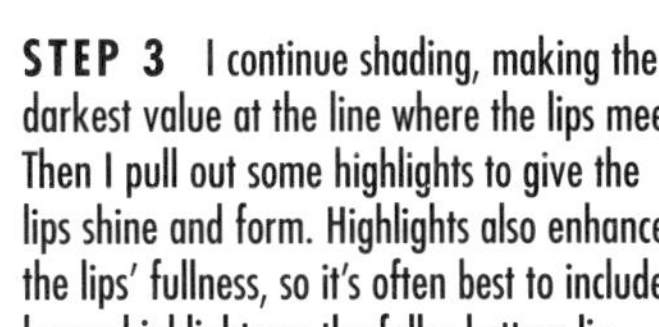

STEP 1 When drawing lips, I first sketch the basic outline. The top lip slightly protrudes over the bottom lip; the bottom lip is also usually fuller than the top lip.

STEP 2 Next I begin shading in the direction of the planes of the lips. The shading on the top lip curves upward, and the shading on the bottom lip curves downward.

STEP 3 I continue shading, making the darkest value at the line where the lips meet. Then I pull out some highlights to give the lips shine and form. Highlights also enhance the lips' fullness, so it's often best to include larger highlights on the fuller bottom lip.

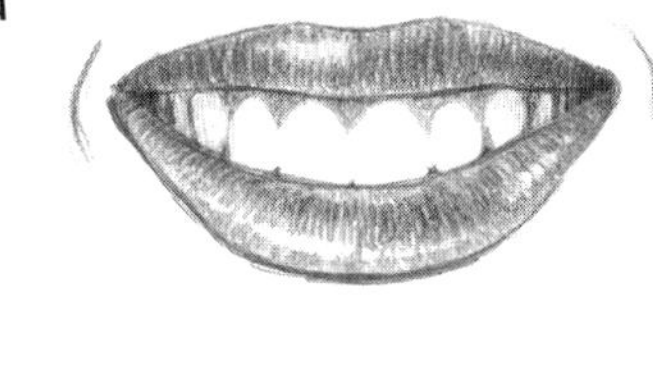

A

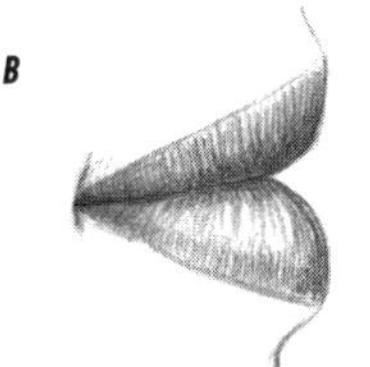

B

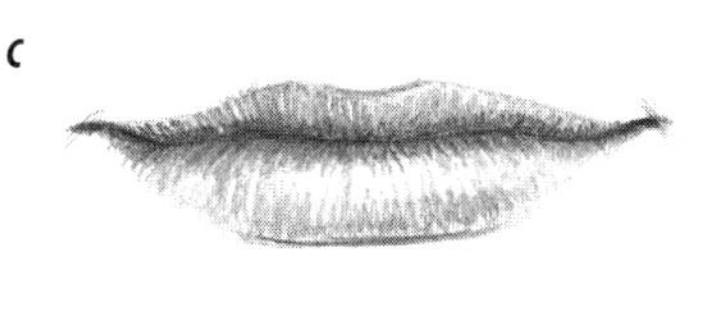

C

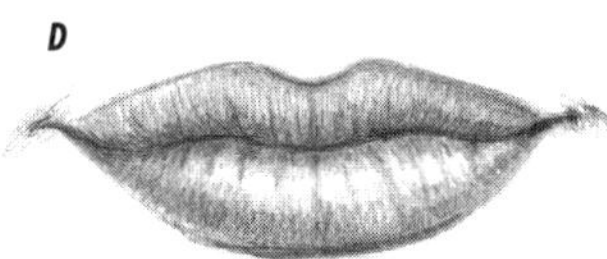

D

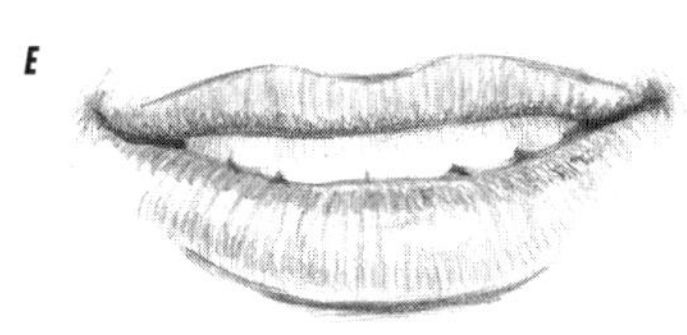

E

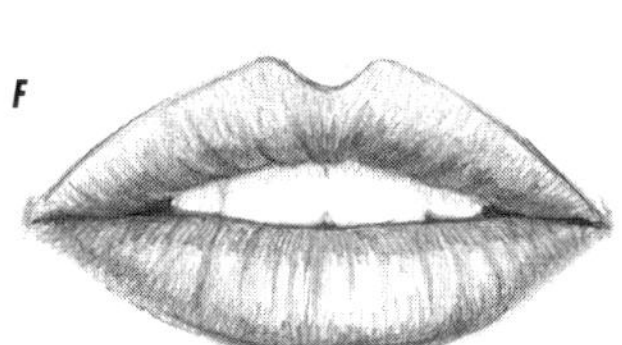

F

DETAILING THE LIPS Determine how much detail you'd like to add to your renderings of lips. You can add smile lines and dimples (A, B, and D), you can draw clearly defined teeth (A) or parts of the teeth (E and F), or you can draw closed lips (B, C, and D).

Combining Features

STEP 1 First I simplify the nose by dividing it into four planes—plus a circle on the tip to indicate its roundness. Then I draw the outline of the lips. I add a small circle to connect the base of the nose with the top of the lip. The arrows on the lips indicate the direction in which I will shade them.

STEP 2 Now I lightly shade the sides of the nose, as well as the nostrils and the area between the nose and lips. I begin shading the lips in the direction indicated by the arrows in step 1. Then I shade the dark area between the top and bottom lips. This helps separate the lips and gives them form.

STEP 3 I continue shading to create the forms of the nose and mouth. Where appropriate, I retain lighter areas for highlights and to show reflected light. For example, I use a kneaded eraser to pull out highlights on the top lip, on the tip of the nose, and on the bridge of the nose.

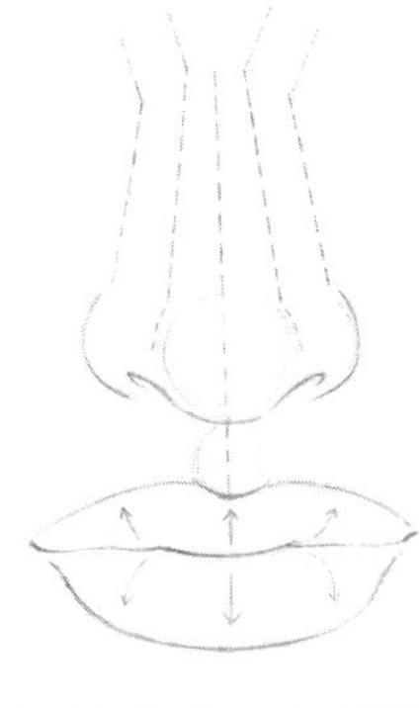

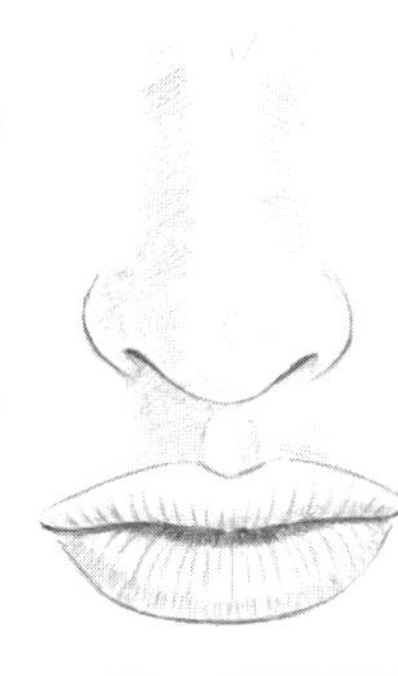

Capturing a Likeness

Once you've practiced drawing the individual features, you're ready to combine them in a full portrait. Use your understanding of the basics of proportion to block in the head and place the features. Study your subject carefully to see how his or her facial proportions differ from the "average"; capturing these subtle differences will help you achieve a better likeness to your subject.

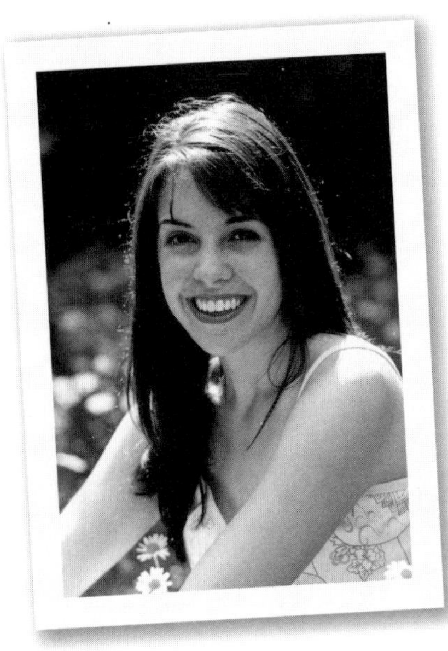

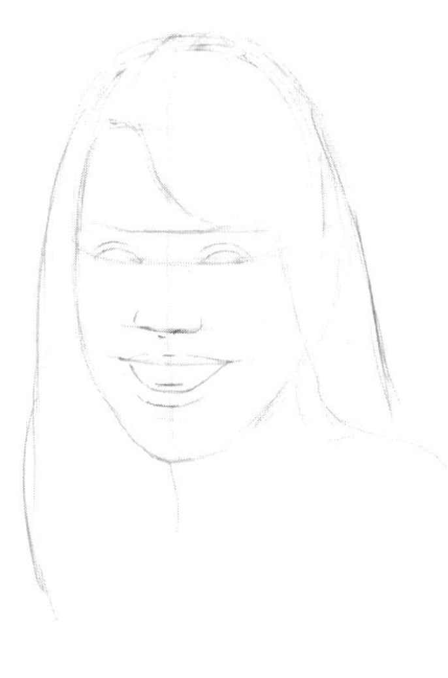

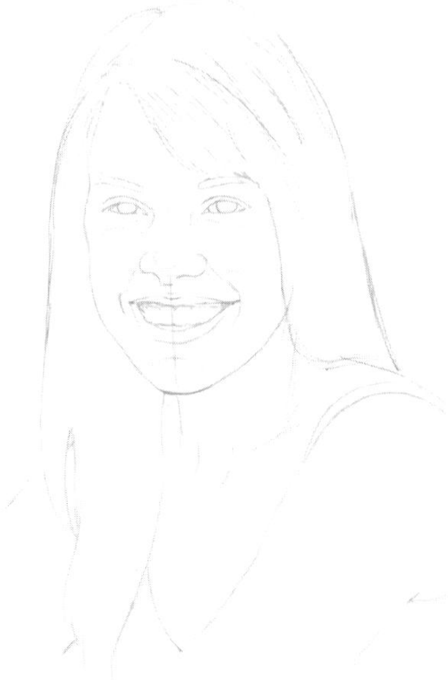

DRAWING WHAT YOU SEE Working from a photo helps you draw what you really see — as opposed to what you expect to see — because you can change your viewpoint. Try turning both the photo and your drawing upside down as you work; you'll find that you can represent many shapes more accurately.

STEP 1 Using an HB pencil, I sketch the general outline of the subject's face. Then I place the facial guidelines before blocking in the eyes, nose, and mouth. (Notice that the mouth takes up about one-fourth of the face.) I also block in the shape of her hair, including the bangs.

STEP 2 Switching to a 2B pencil, I indicate the roundness of the facial features. I compare my sketch to the photograph often, making sure that I've captured the things that make this individual unique, like the turned-up nose, slightly asymmetric eyes, and wide smile.

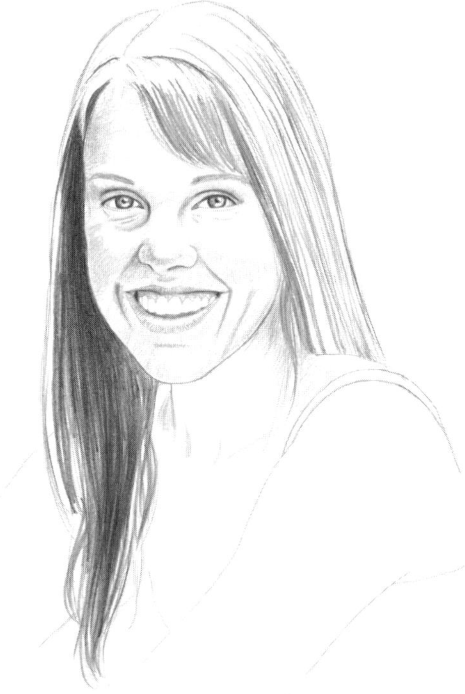

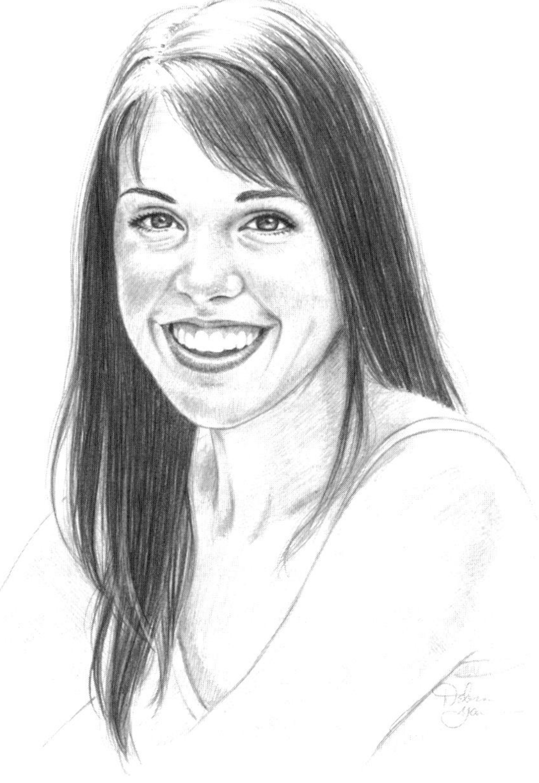

STEP 3 I erase my guidelines and then begin shading, following the form of the face with the 2B pencil and softly blending to create the smoothness of the skin. Next I create the teeth, lightly indicating the separations with incomplete lines. Then I switch to a 3B pencil to lay in more dark streaks of hair.

STEP 4 To render the smooth, shiny hair, I use a 4B to lay in darker values. I vary the length of the strokes, pulling some strokes into the areas at the top of her head that have been left white for highlights to produce a gradual transition from light to dark. Then I refine the eyes and mouth by adding darker layers of shading.

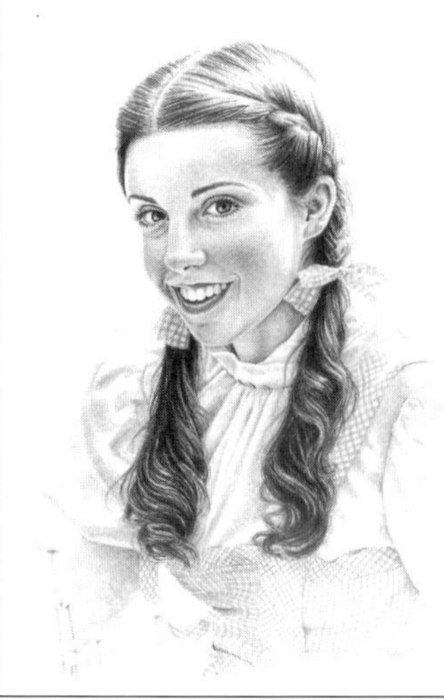

Focusing on Features

This drawing shows the same young lady with a different hair style, expression, and pose. Although she's in costume, she is still recognizable as the same subject because I was faithful to the facial characteristics that are specific to this individual.

Drawing from Life

aving models pose for you as you draw—or drawing from life—is an excellent way to practice rendering faces. When drawing from life, you usually have control over the way your models are lit. If you're indoors, you can position the light source to our liking; if you're outdoors, you can reposition your model until you're satisfied.

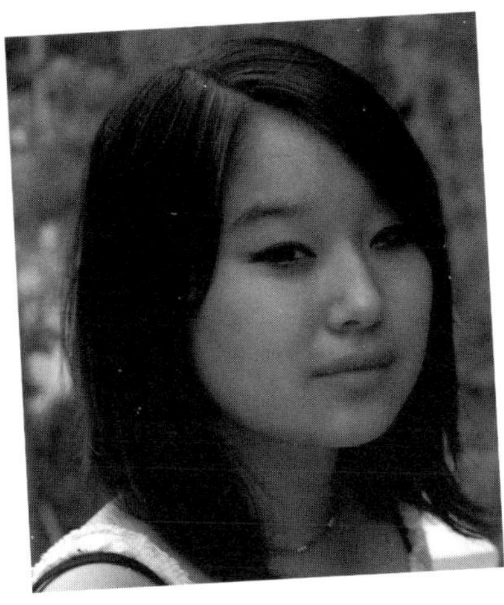

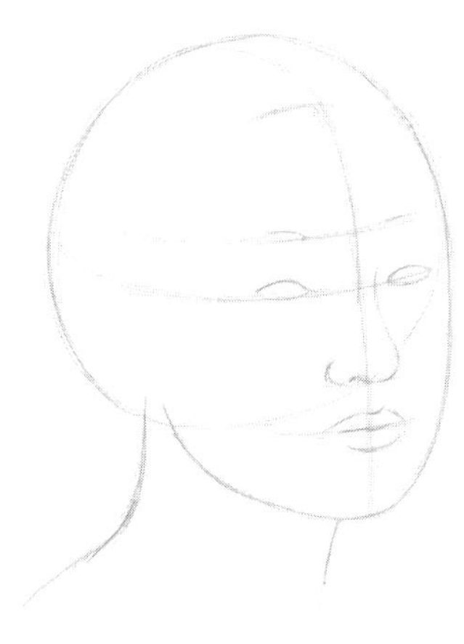

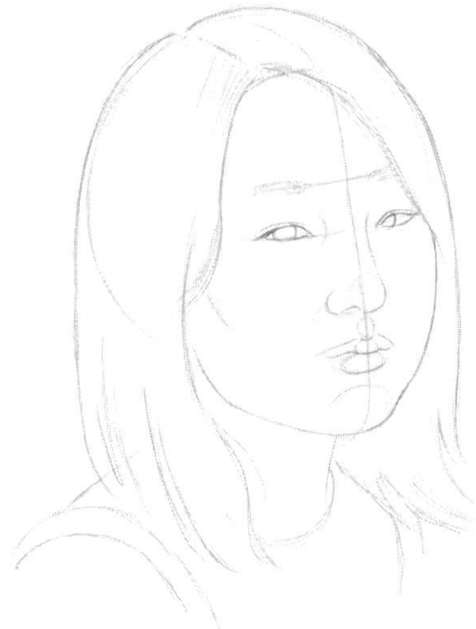

REATING A COMFORTABLE SETUP When using live dels, make sure they are comfortable and in a pose they can d for a while. Schedule short breaks every 30 minutes so that h you and your models can take a "breather."

STEP 1 First I place the basic shape of the head with an HB pencil. My subject's head is tilted at a three-quarter angle, so I shift the vertical centerline to the right a bit. (See page 7 for specific information on placing features in a three-quarter view.) I use my guidelines to block in the eyes, nose, and mouth. Then I indicate the neck.

STEP 2 I use the same HB pencil to foreshorten the subject's left eye, making it a little smaller than the right eye. (See "Shifting the Features" on page 7 for more on foreshortening.) I draw only one nostril, and I make the mouth smaller on the left side. Making closer elements larger shows that the face is angled toward the viewer.

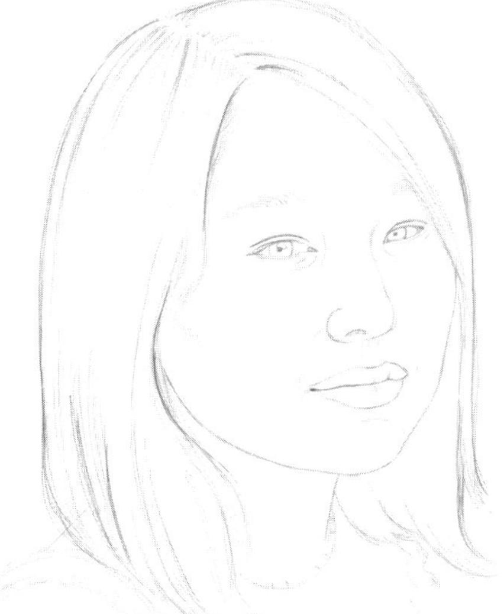

STEP 3 I let my model take a short break so she can relax and stretch while I check the proportions of my drawing. When I'm satisfied with the placement of the features, I begin to develop the eyes, nose, mouth, and eyebrows. I take note of what my model is wearing (her necklace and the ruffled shirt), and begin to render the details accurately.

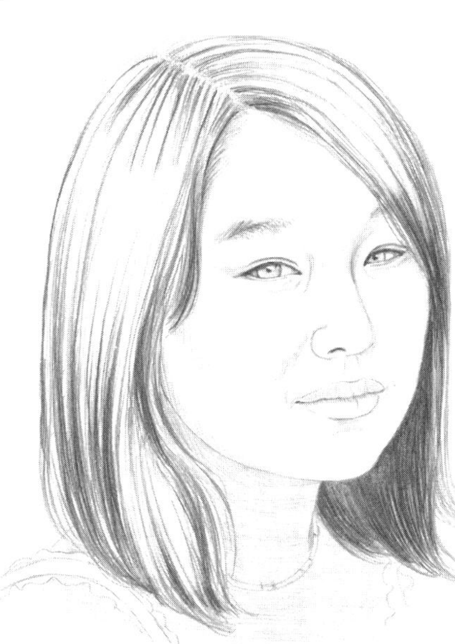

TEP 4 I start shading e face in the darkest areas, quently looking up at my odel to see where the shad- vs lie. I use a 2B pencil to velop the hair, varying the agth of my strokes and aving some areas mostly aite for highlights. Then I ade the neck using light, arizontal strokes.

STEP 5 After another short break, I use a 3B pencil to add even darker values to the hair, leaving the lightest areas at the top of her head to show that the light is coming directly from above. Looking up at my model to locate the lightest values in her face, I use a kneaded eraser to lift out some highlights and to soften any strokes that are too dark, smoothing out the skin.

Approaching a Profile View

A profile view can be very dramatic. Seeing only one side of the face can bring out a subject's distinctive features, such as a protruding brow, an upturned nose, or a strong chin. Because parts of the face appear more prominent in profile, be careful not to allow any one feature to dominate the entire drawing. Take your time working out the proportions before drawing the complete portrait.

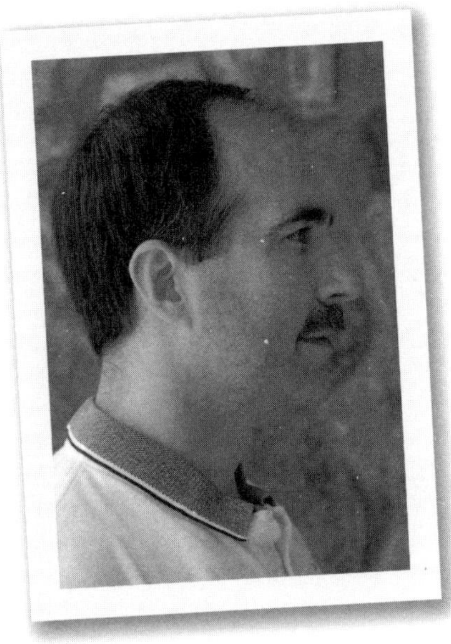

DRAWING IN PROFILE When drawing a subject in profile, be careful with proportions, as your facial guidelines will differ slightly. In a profile view, you see more of the back of the head than you do of the face, so be sure to draw the shape of the skull accordingly.

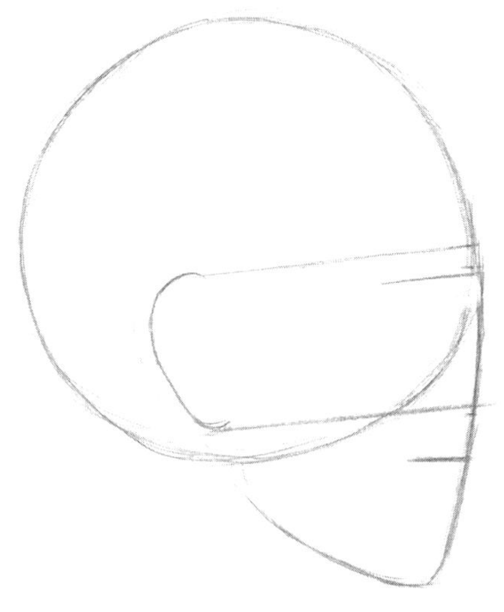

STEP 1 After lightly drawing a circle for the cranial mass, I use an HB pencil to block in the general shapes of the face, chin, and jaw line. Then I add guidelines for the eyes, nose, mouth, and ear. (See page 7 for general rules regarding the placement of features in a profile view.) I closely observe my subject to see how the positions and angles of his features differ from the "average."

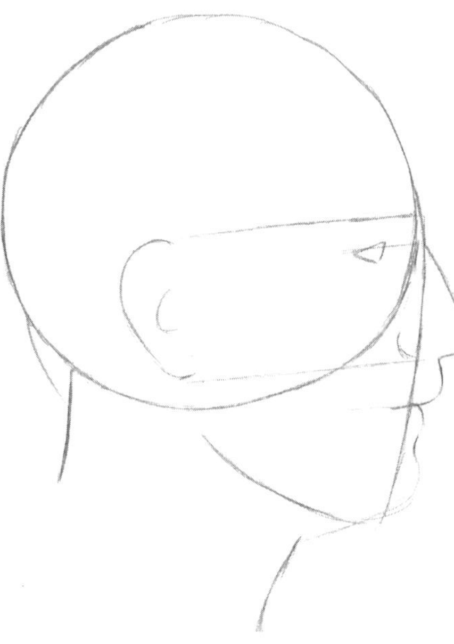

STEP 2 Following the guidelines, I rough in the shapes of the features, including my subject's slightly protruding upper li. I sketch a small part of the eye, indicating how little of the iris you actually see in a profile view. (See page 8 for more information on drawing eyes in profile.)

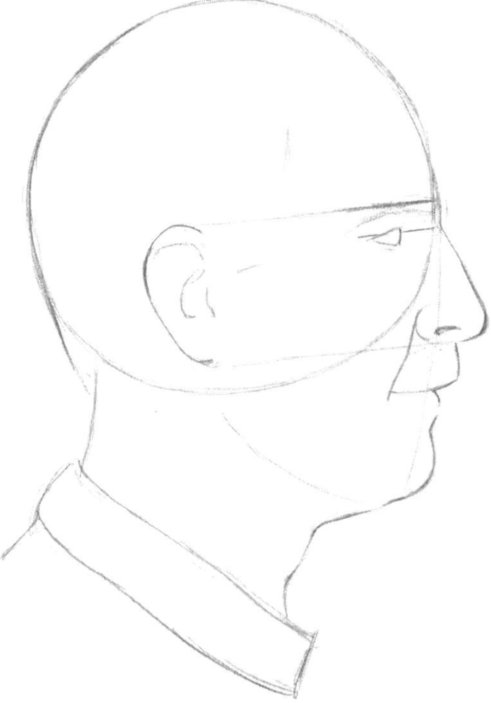

STEP 3 When I sketch the eyebrow, I pay particular attention to the space between the eye and the eyebrow; in this case, the subject's eyebrow is fairly close to his eye. It also grows past the inside corner of his eye, very close to his nose, and tapers toward the outside corner of the eye. Next I continue refining the profile, carefully defining the shapes of the chin and the neck (including the Adam's apple).

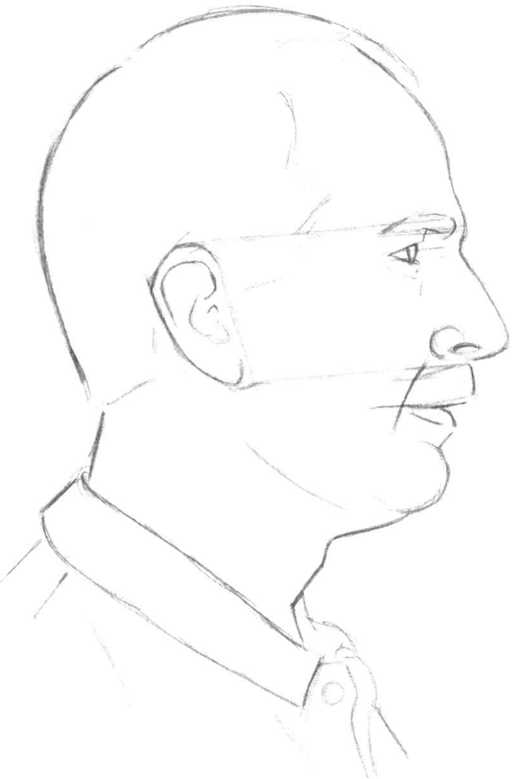

STEP 4 In a profile view, the hairline is important to achieving a likeness, as it affects the size and shape of the forehead. This subject has a very high forehead, so the hairline starts near the vertical centerline of the cranial mass. Once I'm happy with the shapes of the face and hairline, I start refining the features, giving them form.

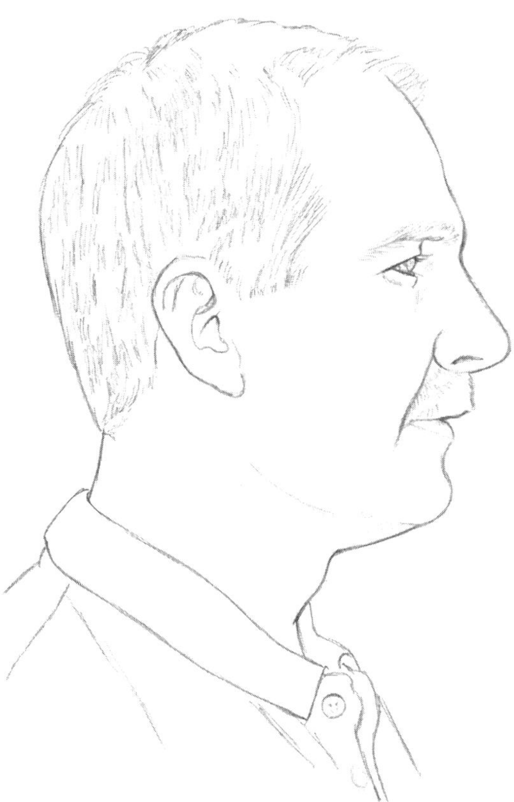

STEP 5 Here you can see that the drawing is really starting to resemble the subject. Next I switch to a 2B pencil and continue building up the forms: I round out the nose and chin; add light, soft strokes to the area above the lip for the mustache; and suggest the hair using short, quick strokes. Then I add more detail to the eye and develop the ear and the eyebrow.

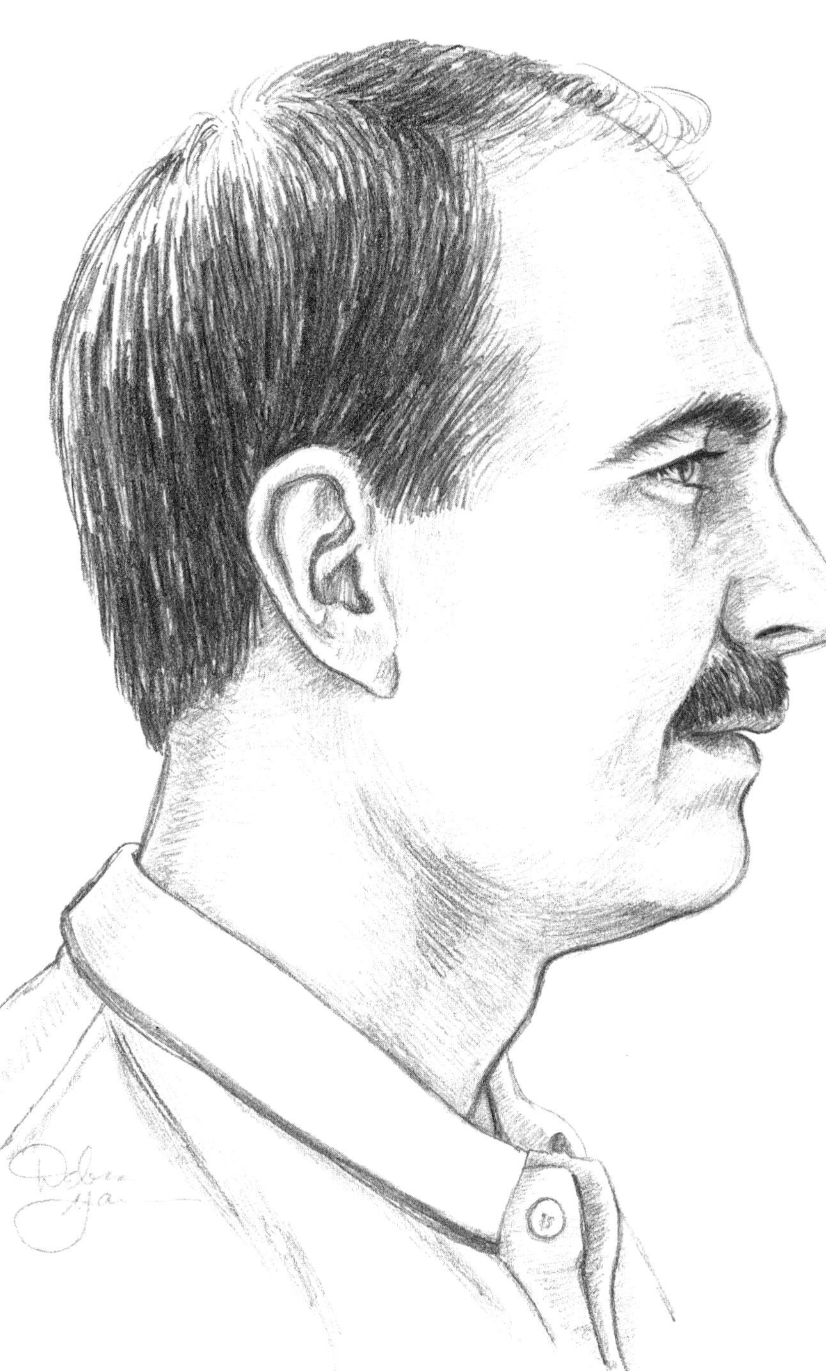

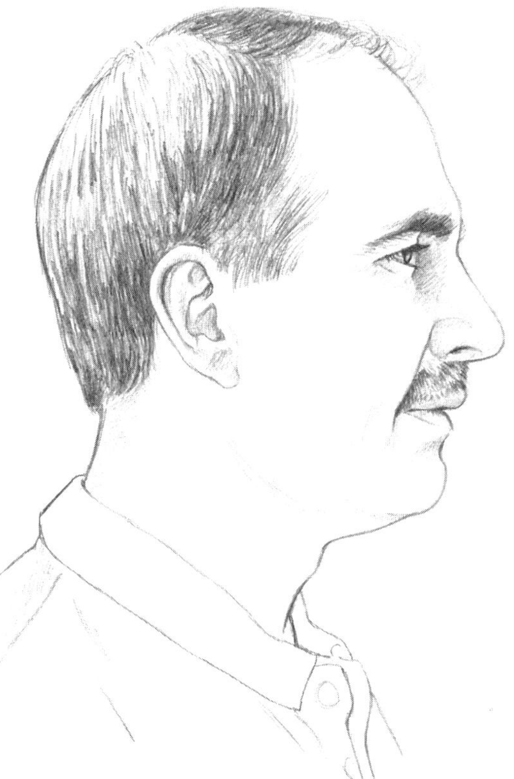

STEP 7 I continue shading the lips, pulling out a white highlight on the bottom lip with a kneaded eraser. Then I shade more of the ear and add even darker values to the hair, leaving highlights on the crown of the head, as it is in the direct path of the light source. I also shade the forehead, the nose, and the chin. I leave the majority of the cheek and the middle part of the forehead white. This helps indicate that the light source is coming from above, angled toward the visible side of the face.

STEP 6 Still using the 2B, I continue to develop the hair, eyebrows, and mustache, always stroking in the direction that the hair grows. I leave plenty of white areas in the hair to create the illusion of individual strands. Next I begin to suggest the curves and shadows of the face by shading the eye, ear, and nose. (See "The Effects of Light" on page 5 for tips on shading a profile.)

Working with Lighting

Whether you're drawing from a photo or from life, lighting is extremely important to the overall feeling of your portrait. Lighting can influence the mood or atmosphere of your drawing—intense lighting creates drama, whereas soft lighting produces a more tranquil feeling. Lighting can also affect shadows, creating stronger contrasts between light and dark values. Remember that the lightest highlights will be in the direct path of your light source, and the darkest shadows will be opposite the light source.

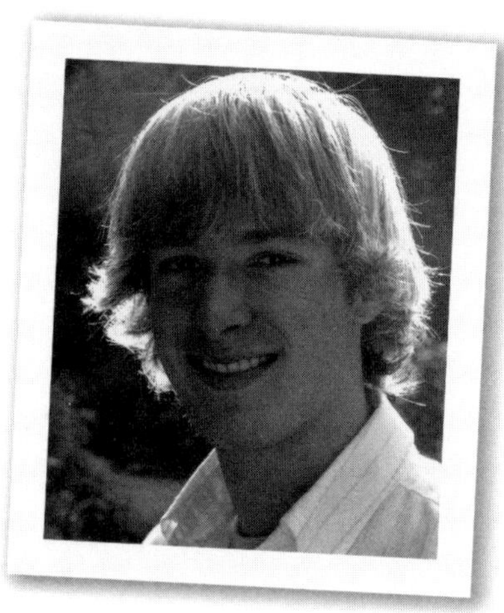

USING BACKLIGHTING   Here the light source is coming from behind the subject—the face is in shadow, but the hair is highlighted. When drawing a backlit subject, try leaving some areas of paper white around the edges of the head. This keeps the hair from looking stiff and unrealistic, and it also separates the hair from the background.

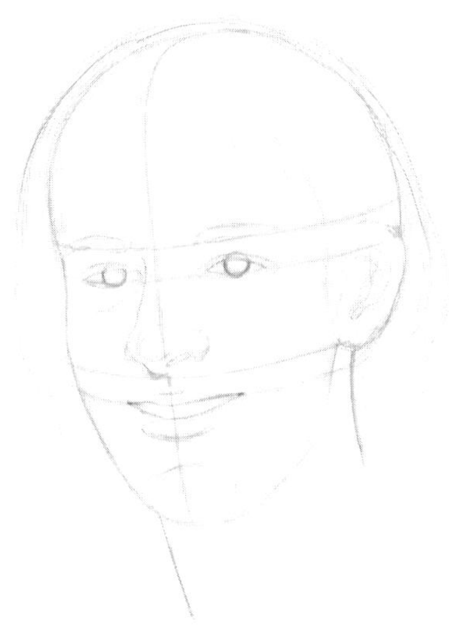

STEP 1   I sketch the basic shape of the head, neck, and hair with an HB pencil. My subject's head is turned in a three-quarter view, so I curve the guidelines around the face accordingly. (See page 7.) Then I lightly sketch the facial features, indicating the roundness of the nose and the chin.

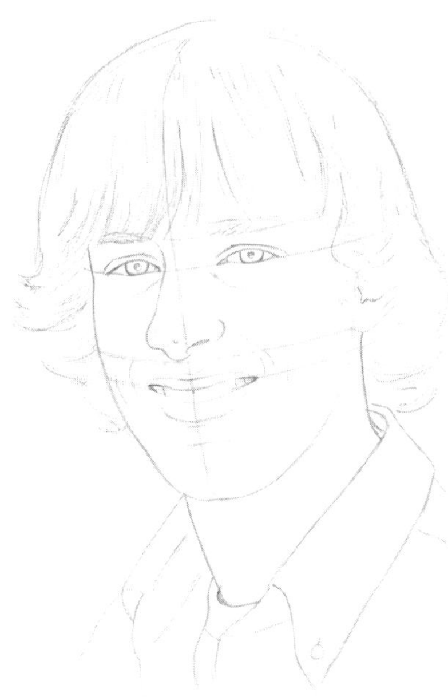

STEP 2   Switching to a 2B pencil, I define the features and fill in the eyebrows. I also sketch a few creases near the mouth and around the eyes. Then I add the collar, button, and neckband to his shirt.

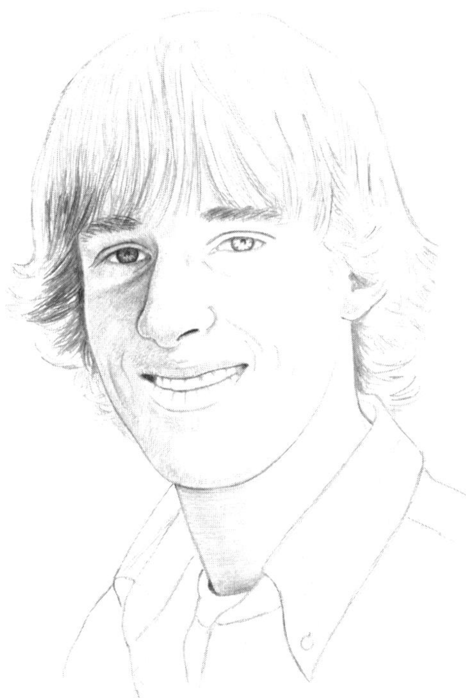

STEP 3   Using a 2B and frequently referring to my photograph, I shade the right side of the face: First I apply a layer of light, short strokes; then I go back and apply a layer of longer strokes, still maintaining a light touch. To shade the hair, I leave several white areas to indicate that the light is shining through it. I apply long strokes, staggering them at the top of the head to produce an uneven, more realistic shape.

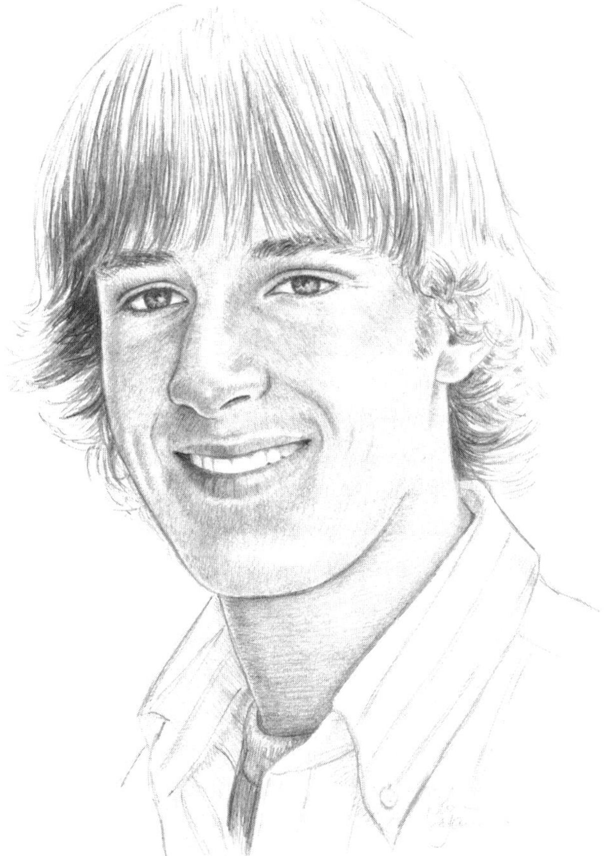

STEP 4   Still using a 2B pencil, I continue shading the face, keeping the left side a bit lighter in value to show that the light source is coming from the subject's left. I also refine the left eye, leaving the right eye more in shadow. I shade the neck, again making his right side a bit darker. Then I add more definition to the hair, leaving some white space around the edges to suggest the light shining through the hair.

Including a Background

n effective background will draw the viewer's eye to your subject and play a role in setting a mood. A background should ways complement a drawing; it should never overwhelm the subject. Generally a light, neutral setting will enhance a subject with dark hair skin, and a dark background will set off a subject with light hair or skin.

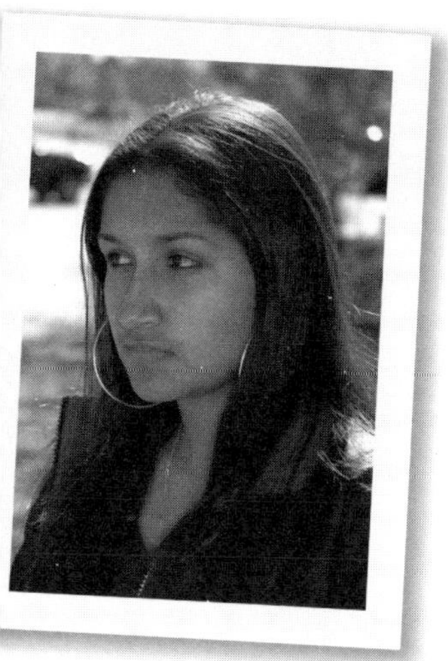

MPLIFYING A BACKGROUND en working from a photo reference that features unflattering background, you can easily change Simplify a background by removing any extra- us elements or altering the overall values.

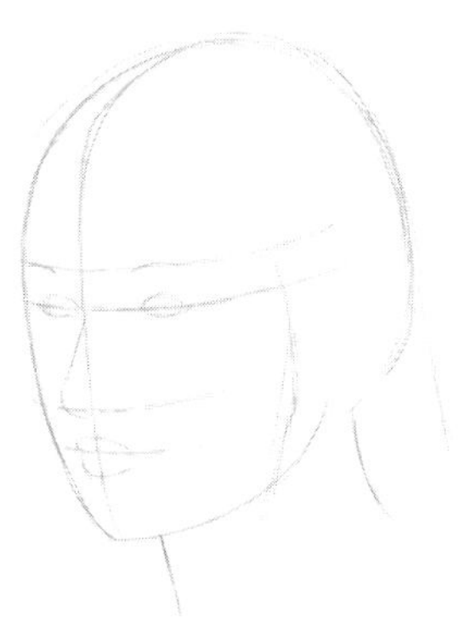

STEP 1 With an HB pencil, I sketch in the basic head shape and the guidelines. Then I block in the position of the eyes, brows, nose, and mouth. (Notice that the center guideline is to the far left of the face because of the way the head is turned.) Next I indicate the neck and the hair.

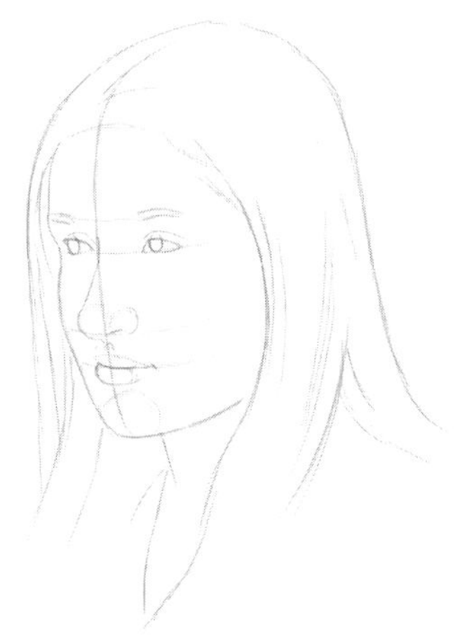

STEP 2 Switching to a 2B pencil, I begin refining the shape of the eyes, brows, nose, and mouth. I block in the hair with long, sweeping strokes, curving around the face and drawing in the direction the hair grows. Then I add a neckline to her shirt.

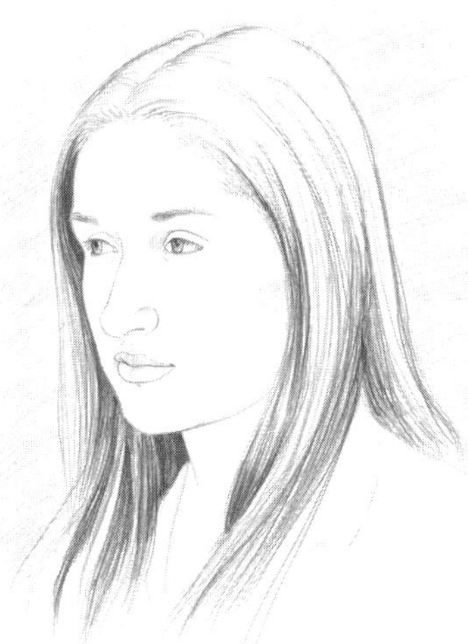

STEP 3 First I shade the irises with a 2B pencil. Then I begin shading the background using diagonal hatching strokes. Once the back-ground is laid in, I use a 3B to build up the dark values of the hair. (I create the background before developing the hair so my hand doesn't smear the delicate strands of hair.)

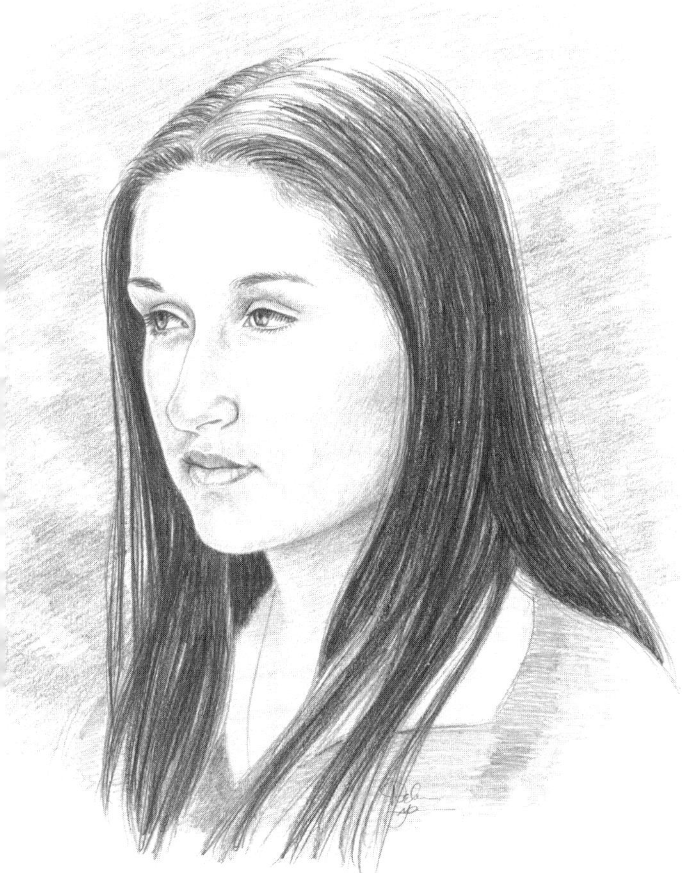

EP 4 I finish shading the face, neck, and shirt with a 2B; then I switch to a 3B to add more k streaks to the hair. I apply another layer of strokes to the background, carefully working und the hair and leaving a few gaps between the strokes to create texture and interest. Next I a kneaded eraser to smooth out the transitions.

Creating Drama

A darker background can add intensity or drama to your portrait. Here the subject is in profile, so the lightest values of her face stand out against the dark values of the background. To ensure that her dark hair does not become "lost," I create a gradation from dark to light, leaving the lightest areas of the background at the top and along the edge of the hair for separation.

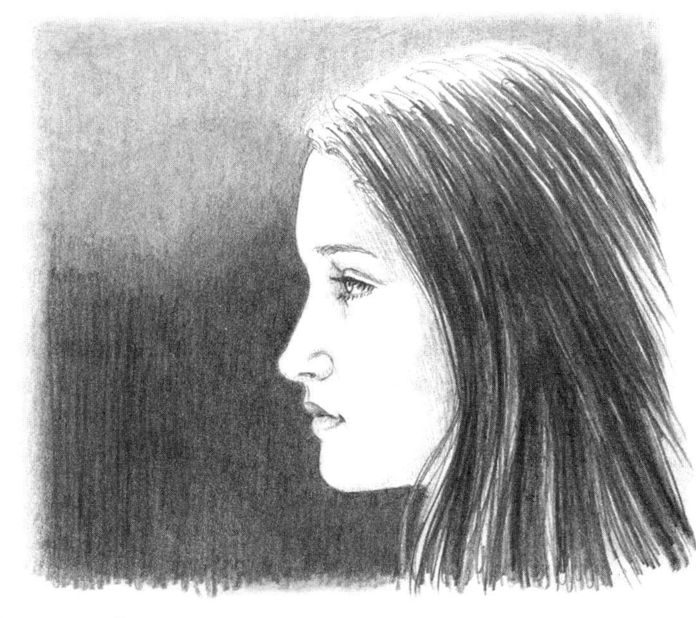

Developing Hair

There are many different types and styles of hair—thick and thin; long and short; curly, straight, and wavy; and even braided! And because hair is often one of an individual's most distinguishing features, knowing how to render different types and textures is essential. When drawing hair, don't try to draw every strand; just create the overall impression and allow the viewer's eye and imagination to fill in the rest.

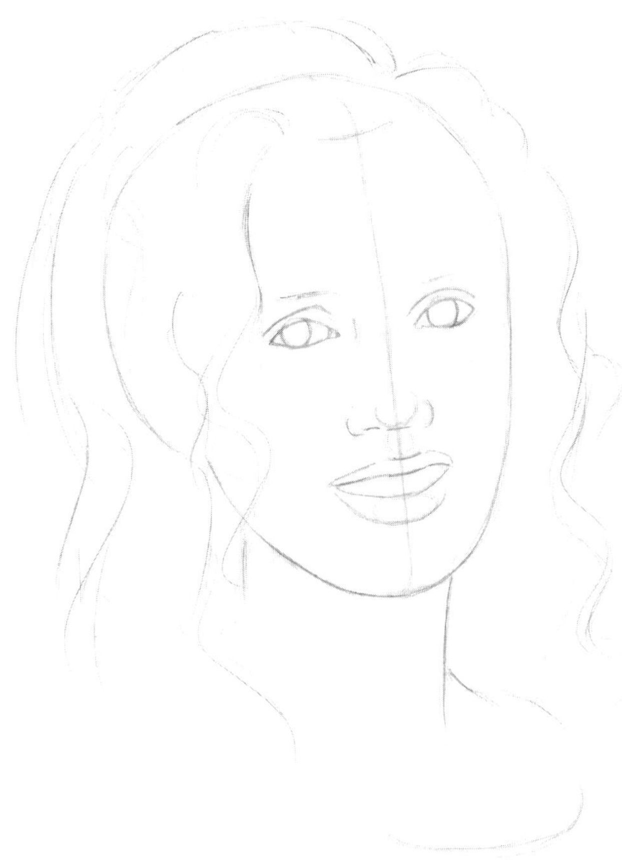

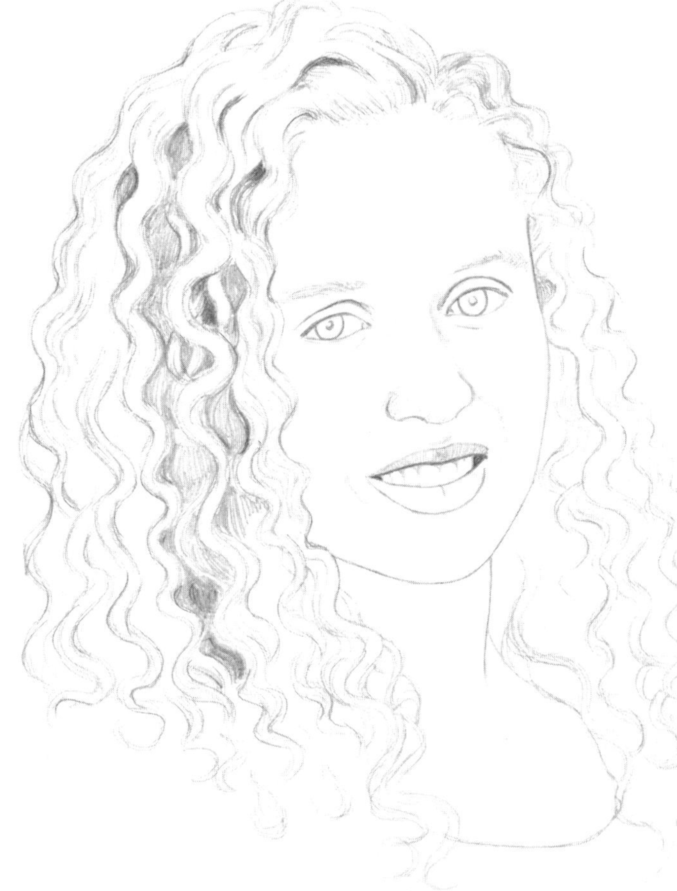

STEP 1 I use an HB pencil to sketch the shape of the head and place the features. Then I use loose strokes to block in the general outline of the hair. Starting at the part on the left side of the head, I lightly draw the hair in the direction of growth on either side of the part. At this stage, I merely indicate the shape of the hair; I don't worry about the individual ringlets yet.

STEP 2 Switching to a 2B pencil, I start refining the eyes, eyebrows, nose, and mouth. Then I define the neckline of her shirt with curved lines that follow the shape of her body. Returning to the hair, I lightly sketch in sections of ringlets, working from top to bottom. I start adding dark values underneath and behind certain sections of hair, creating contrast and depth. (See "Creating Ringlets" below.)

Creating Ringlets

STEP 1 First I sketch the shapes of the ringlets using curved, S-shaped lines. I make sure that the ringlets are not too similar in shape—some are thick and some are thin.

STEP 2 To give the ringlets form, I squint my eyes to find the dark and light values. I leave the top of the ringlets (the hair closest to the head) lighter and add a bit more shading as I move down the strands, indicating that the light is coming from above.

STEP 3 To create the darkest values underneath the hair, I place the strokes closer together.

STEP 4 I add even darker values, making sure that my transitions in value are smooth and that there are no abrupt changes in direction.

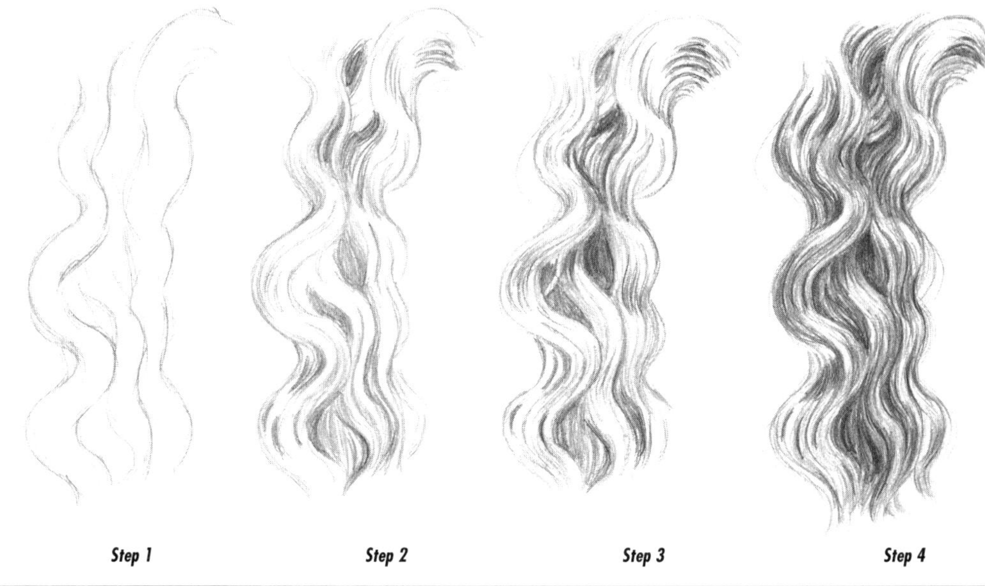

Step 1 *Step 2* *Step 3* *Step 4*

STEP 3 I shade the face, neck,
and chest using linear strokes that
reach across the width of the body.
Then I define the eyes, lips, and
teeth, and I add her shoulder and
the sleeve of her shirt. Next I continue working in darker values
within the ringlets, leaving some
areas of hair white to suggest
and highlights. Although the hair
is much more detailed at this final
stage, I am still simply indicating
the general mass, allowing the
viewer's eye to complete the
scene. Finally I draw some loose
strands along the edges of the
hair, leaving the lightest values
at the top of the subject's head.

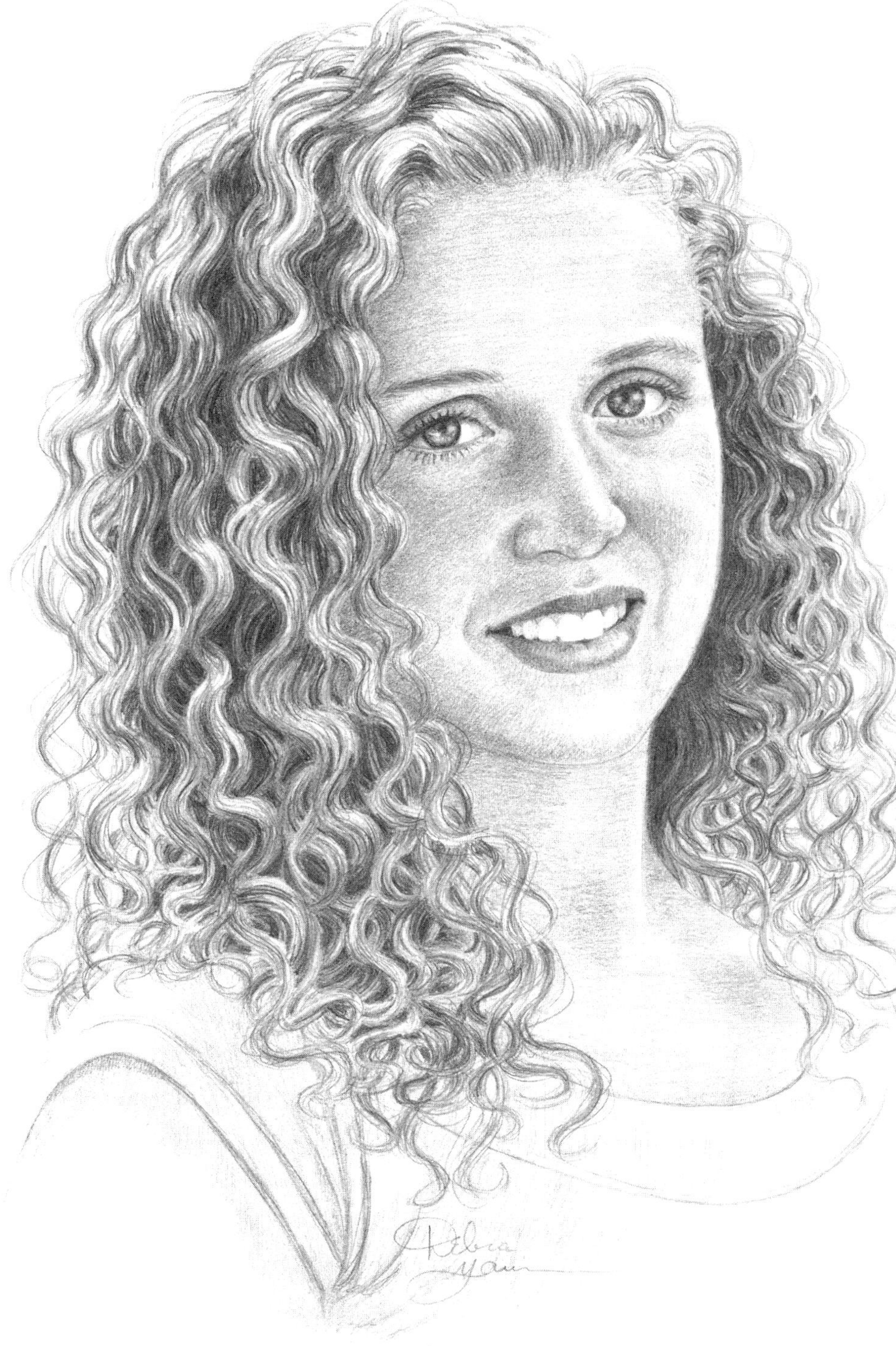

Rendering Braids

STEP 1 First I sketch the outline of each braid. I
taper the ends a bit, adding a line across the bottom of
each to indicate the ties that hold the braids together.

STEP 2 Now I start shading each section, indicating
the overlapping hair in each braid. I add some wispy
hair "escaping" from the braids to add realism.

STEP 3 I continue shading the braids using heavier
strokes. I add even more "escaped" strands of hair. Then
I use a kneaded eraser to pull out highlights at the bottom of each braid, emphasizing the ties. I also pull out
some highlights in the braids themselves.

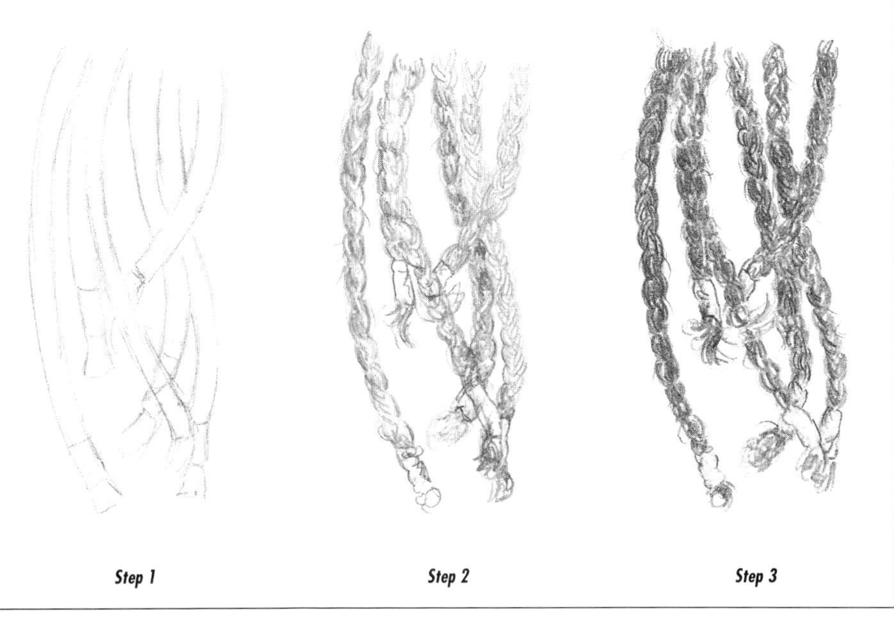

Depicting Age

As people age, their skin loses elasticity, causing loose, wrinkled skin; drooping noses; and sagging ears. In addition, lips often become thinner, hair turns gray, and eyesight becomes poor (which is why many elderly subjects wear glasses). Accurately rendering these characteristics is essential to creating successful portraits of mature subjects.

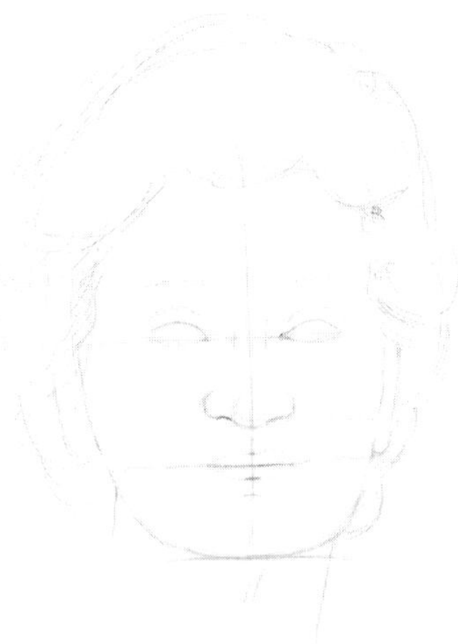

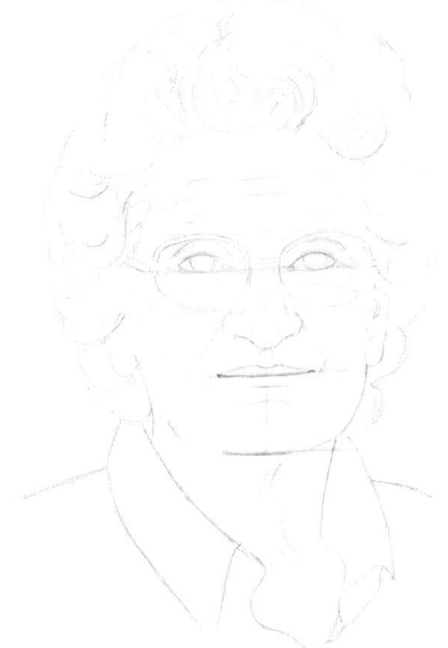

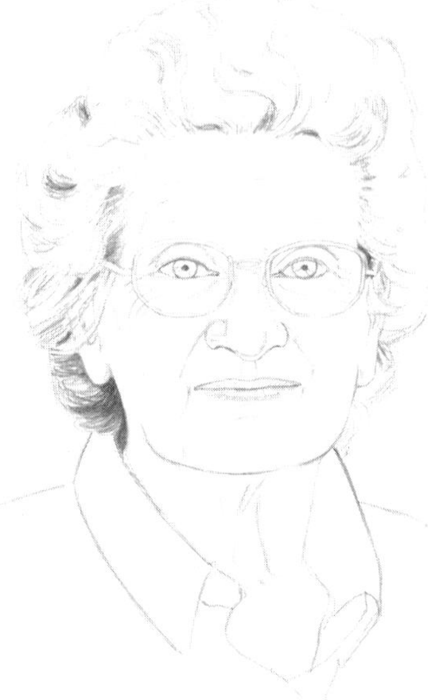

STEP 1   I block in the face with an HB pencil. Then I add guidelines, which I use to place the eyes, nose, ears, eyebrows, and mouth. The lips thin out and move inward as a person ages, so I draw them accordingly. I also sketch the wavy outline of the hair.

STEP 2   I draw the basic shape of the eyeglasses, then begin to suggest my subject's age by adding delicate lines around her eyes and across her forehead. I also round out the jaw and chin to show where the skin has begun to sag. I draw loose skin on the neck and deep lines on either side of the nose.

STEP 3   Switching to a 2B pencil, I begin shading the hair and developing the eyes, adding light, curved lines around and under the eyes to create "bags." I magnify the wrinkles slightly where they can be seen through the glasses. (See "Rendering Wrinkles" below.)

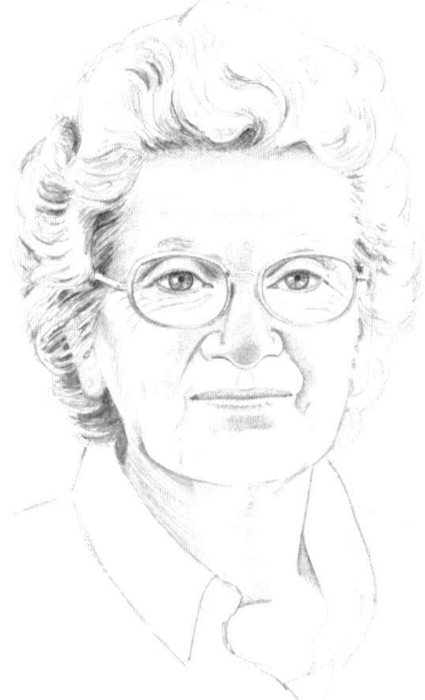

STEP 4   Still using a 2B, I shade the face and neck, adding strokes to the side of the neck for wrinkles. I finish shading the irises and the eyelids. I shade the area between the right side of the cheek and the jawbone to show the prominent cheekbone, and I add shading around the nose and mouth to make the skin appear puffy. Then I add darker values to the hair and earrings.

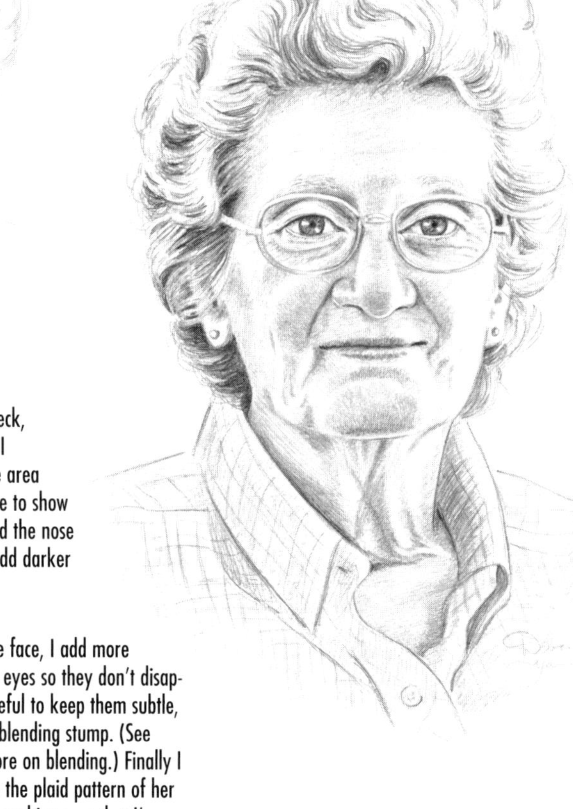

STEP 5   As I continue shading the face, I add more definition to the wrinkles around the eyes so they don't disappear into the shaded areas. I am careful to keep them subtle, smoothing out the transitions with a blending stump. (See "Rendering Wrinkles" at right for more on blending.) Finally I add a button to her collar and create the plaid pattern of her shirt. I stand back from the drawing, making sure that I'm pleased with the effect the angular bones, loose skin, and wrinkles have on the subject's face and that they suggest her age.

Rendering Wrinkles

The key to drawing realistic-looking wrinkles is to keep them subtle. Indicate wrinkles with soft shading, not with hard or angular lines. You can best achieve this effect by using a dull pencil point. You also can use a cloth or a blending stump to softly blend the transitions between the light and dark values in the wrinkles. Or use a kneaded eraser to soften wrinkles that appear too deep.

When drawing a subject with glasses, as in the example below, try to magnify the wrinkle lines that are seen through the lenses. You can do this by drawing the lines of shading a little larger and spacing them farther from one another.

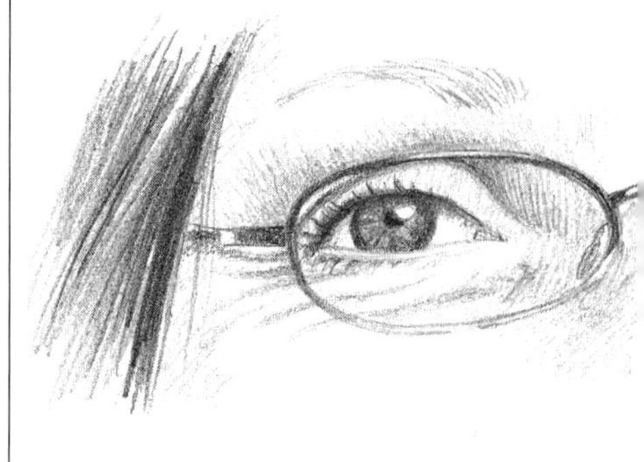

Creating Facial Hair

acial hair is another characteristic that distinguishes one individual from the next. Short, dark strokes are perfect for rendering a thick, coarse beard; whereas light, sweeping strokes are ideal for depicting a wispy mustache. Experiment with variations of light and dark lines when drawing a "salt-and-pepper" beard, and use a series of quick, short lines when indicating stubble.

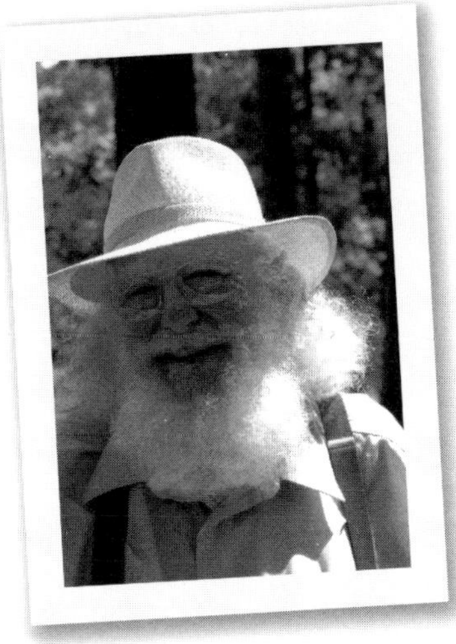

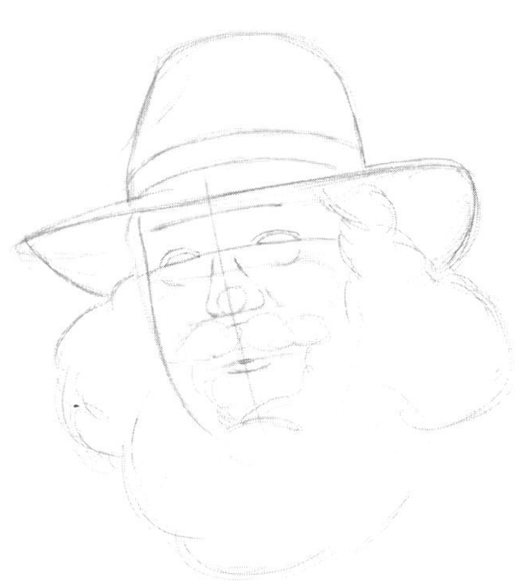

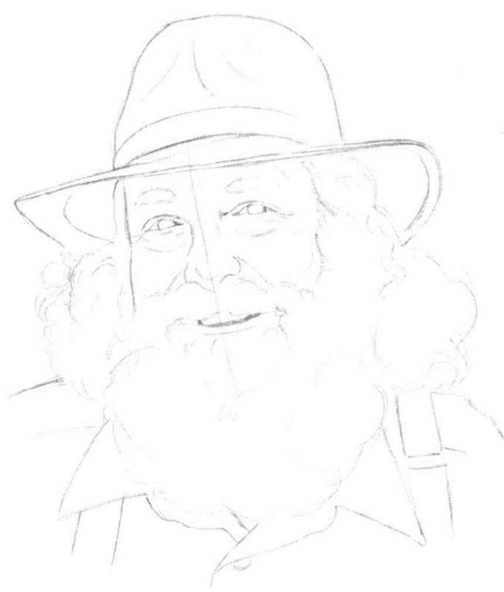

RAWING THROUGH When drawing a face that is partly hidden by facial hair, it is important to draw the entire head first (or "draw through") and then add the hair, beard, and accessories (such as the hat). Although the entire head isn't visible, it still needs to be drawn accurately so the hat sits properly.

STEP 1 First I sketch the shape of the face with an HB pencil. Then I place the guidelines and the features. Next I draw the hat, including the band. I block in the masses of the hair, mustache, and beard with loose, curved lines. Just as when drawing any other type of hair, I simply indicate the general shapes at this stage.

STEP 2 Switching to a 2B pencil, I refine the eyes, eyebrows, and teeth. I add wrinkles around the eyes and on the forehead; then I build up the hat, sketch the shirt collar, and draw the suspenders. Now I return to the hair, indicating the curls with circular strokes. Working from top to bottom, I fill out the top of the hair, and then I develop the mustache, which partially covers the mouth.

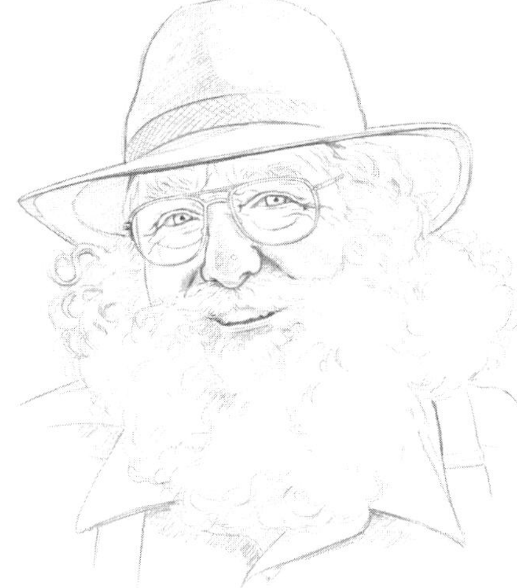

STEP 3 After erasing my guidelines, adding the glasses, and defining the eyes, I shade the hat, cross-hatching (see page 3) to create a pattern on the band. I begin rendering the short, tight curls of the beard and the mustache. Then I add darker values to the curls on the left side of the face to separate them and to show the cast shadow of the hat.

Focusing on Beards

When drawing a white beard, such as this one, group several lines together to create form, but leave some areas white. Also try drawing the strokes in varying directions—this adds interest and movement. It's also a good idea to overlap your shading a bit where the skin meets the hair, indicating that the skin is showing through the beard.

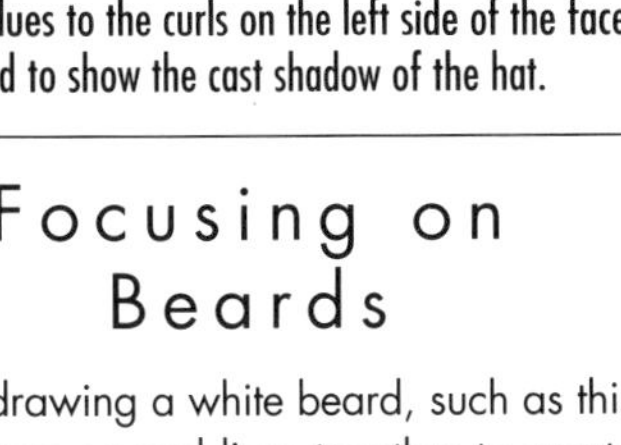

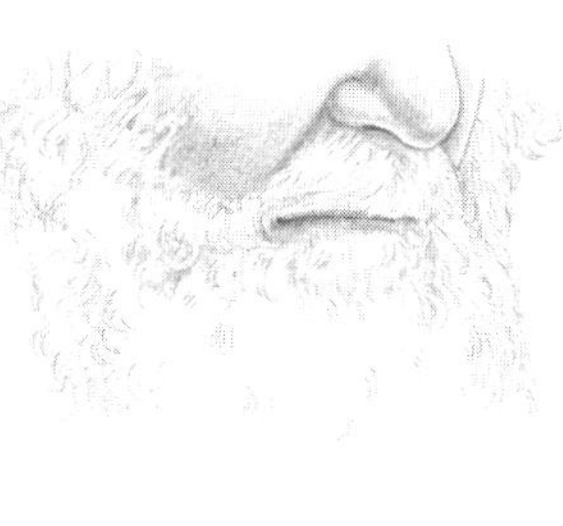

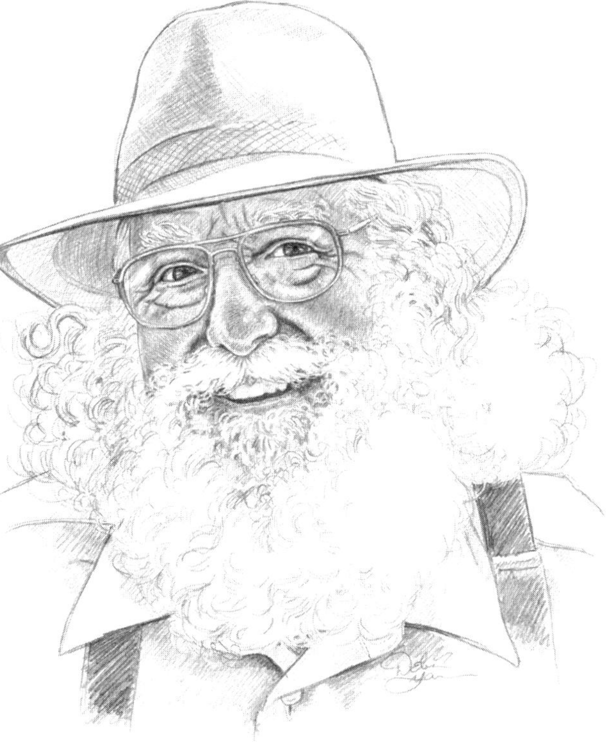

STEP 4 I add a layer of shading to the irises, leaving white highlights in each eye. Using the edge of a kneaded eraser, I pull out a highlight on each lens of the glasses to show the reflected light. I apply more shading to the hat to give it more of a three-dimensional look; then I shade the suspenders and the shirt. Finally I finish the curls in the hair and beard, varying my strokes between tight, curved lines and quick, straight lines. I create the shortest, most defined lines in the mustache and around the mouth, leaving most of the beard to the viewer's imagination.

Understanding Children's Proportions

Children's proportions are different than those of adults: Young children have rounder faces with larger eyes that are spaced farther apart. Their features are also positioned a little lower on the face; for example, the eyebrows begin on the centerline, where the eyes would be on a teenager or an adult. As a child ages, the shape of the face elongates, altering the proportions.

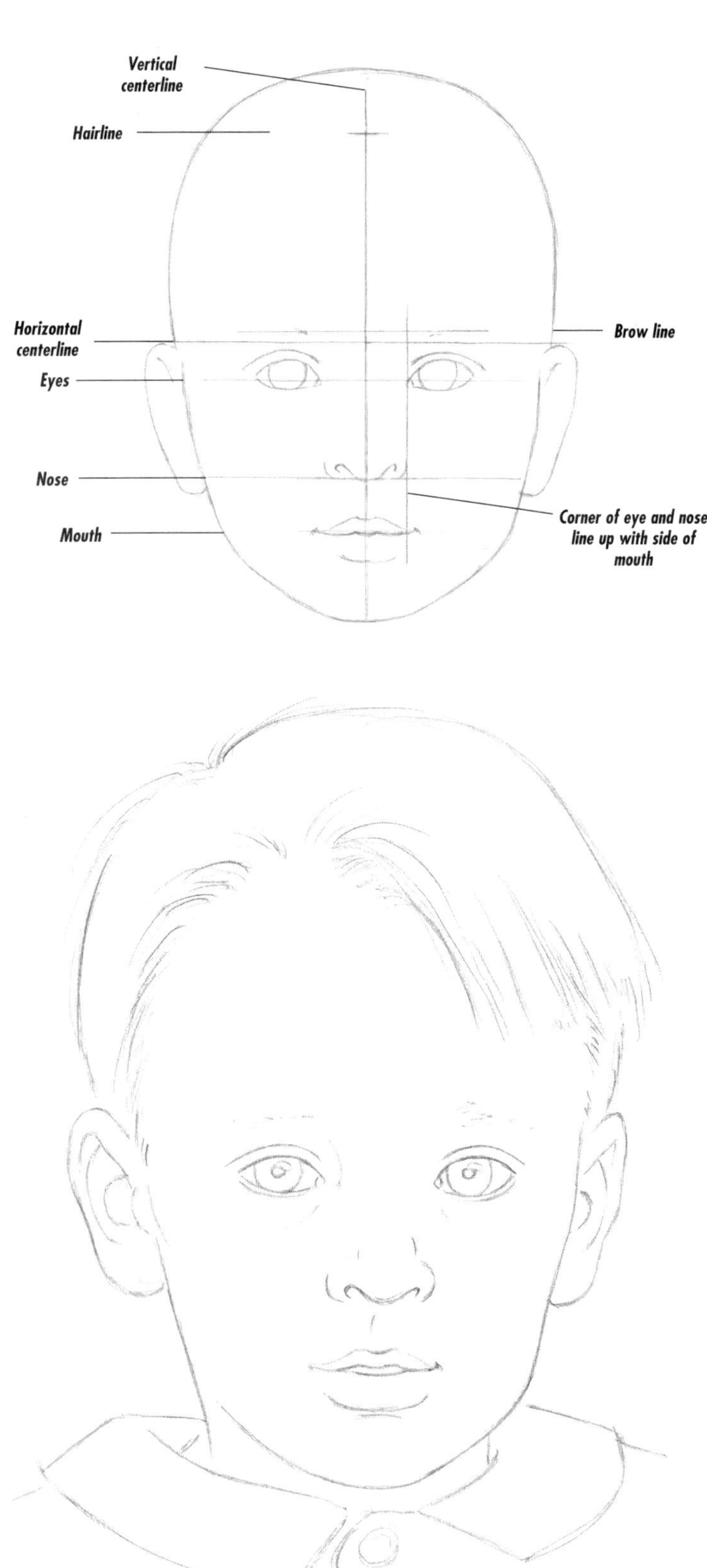

PLACING THE FEATURES Based on the placement of this subject's features, you can estimate that he is around five or six years old. The face has elongated enough to shift the brow line so that it lines up with the tops of the ears, showing that the child is no longer a baby. But the eyes are spaced farther apart, indicating youth. The mouth is still relatively close to the chin, which also emphasizes his young age. (See the diagrams at right for more on the shifting of the features with age.)

Changing Over Time

The placement of the features changes as the face becomes longer and thinner with age. Use horizontal guidelines to divide the area from the horizontal centerline to the chin into equal sections; these lines can then be used to determine where to the place the facial features.

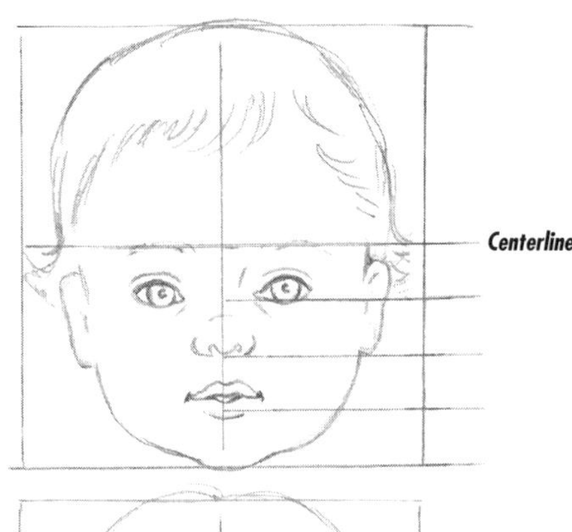

DRAWING AN INFANT A baby's head fits into a square shape, as shown here. Babies have larger foreheads than adults do, so their eyebrows (not their eyes) fall on the horizontal centerline. Their eyes are large in relation to the rest of their features because the eyes are already fully developed at birth.

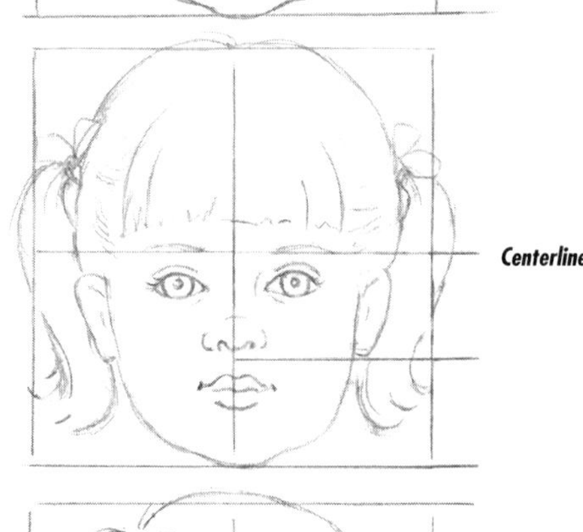

DRAWING A TODDLER As a child grows, the forehead shortens a bit and the chin elongates, so the bottoms of the eyebrows now meet the horizontal centerline. The eyes are still more than one eye-width apart, but they are bit closer together than an infant's eyes are.

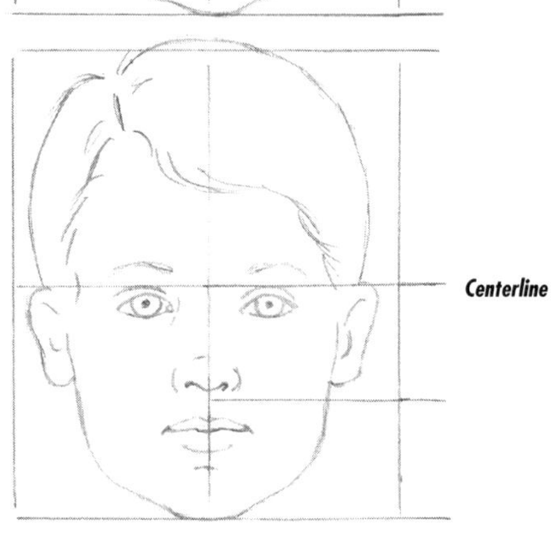

DRAWING A CHILD As a child nears seven or eight years of age, the face has lengthened and fits into more of a rectangular shape. The eyebrows are now well above the horizontal centerline and the eyes are a little closer to the centerline. The ears line up with the bottom of the nose.

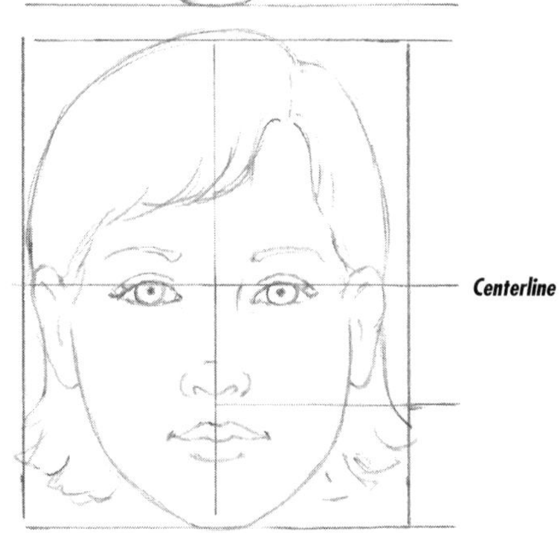

DRAWING A TEENAGER By age 13, the face is even longer and has lost most of its round shape; now it's more oval. The eyes are nearly at the centerline, as on an adult's face, but a teen's face and eyes are still slightly more rounded and full. The tops of the ears are about even with the eyebrows.

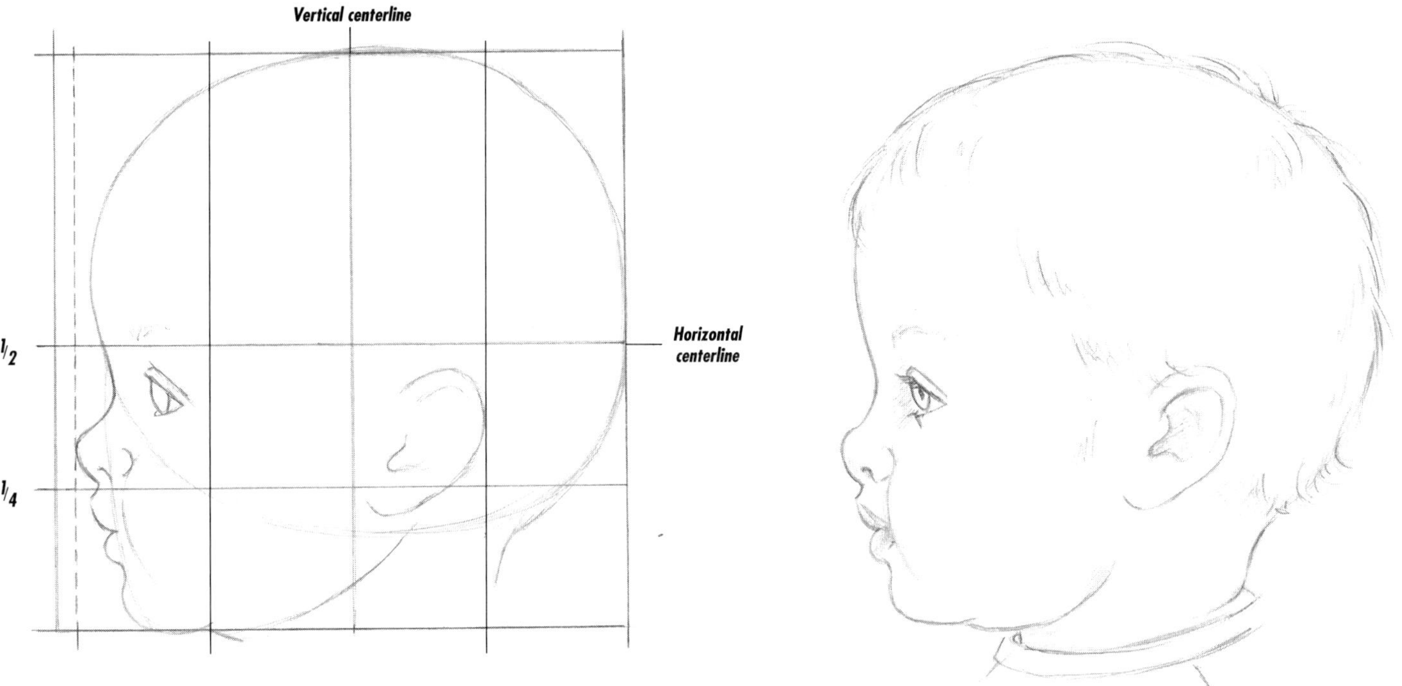

DRAWING A BABY IN PROFILE The profile of a child is usually very rounded. Youngsters generally have bigger, more protruding foreheads than adults do. And children's eyes tend to be smaller and more rounded, as well. The shape of a baby's head in profile also fits into a square.

Block in the large cranial mass with a circle; then sketch the features. The brow line is at the horizontal centerline, whereas the nose is about one-fourth of the way up the face. Study where each feature falls in relation to the dividing lines. In addition, light eyebrows and wispy hair help indicate a baby's age; as children get older, their hair grows in thicker.

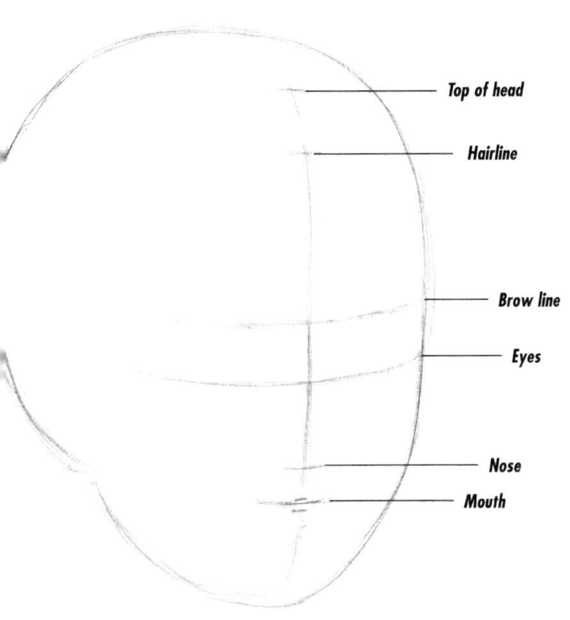

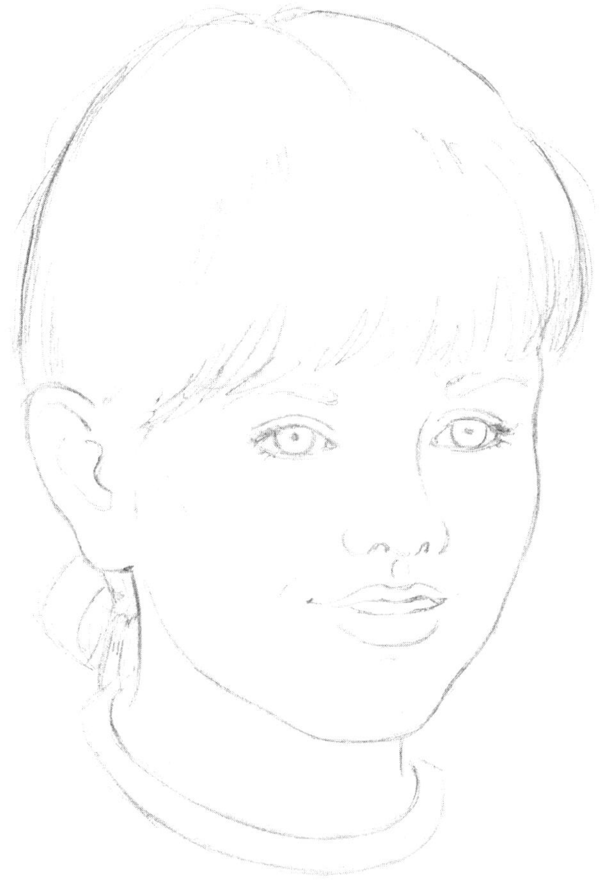

ADDING CHILDREN'S DETAILS The features shift slightly in a three-quarter view, as shown here. Although a baby's features are placed differently on the head than an older child's are, their facial guidelines shift similarly, following the direction in which the head turns. Place the features according to the guidelines. Hair style and clothing — including accessories — can also influence the perceived age of your subject!

Modifying the Profile

As children age, their profiles change quite a bit. The head elongates at each stage: The top of the baby's eyebrow lines up with the bottom of the toddler's eyebrow, the midway-point between the young boy's eyebrow and eyelid, and the top of the teenage girl's eyelid.

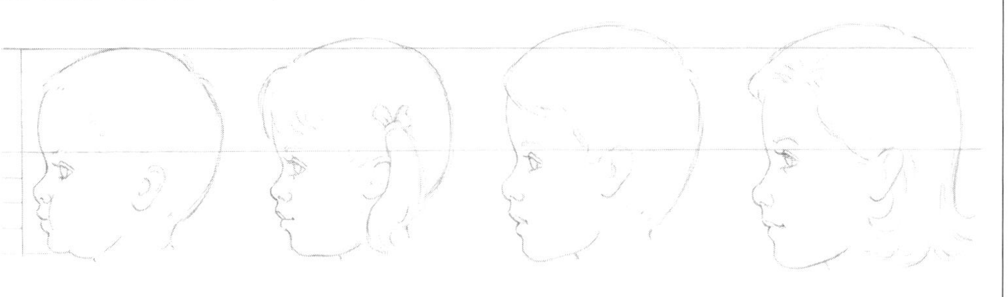

Portraying Children's Features

Children are fascinating drawing subjects, but they can be a challenge to draw accurately. It's important to get the right proportions for the particular age (see pages 20–21 for more on children's proportions) and to correctly render their features: Their eyes tend to be bigger and more rounded than those of adults, their nostrils are barely visible, and their hair is usually fine and wispy.

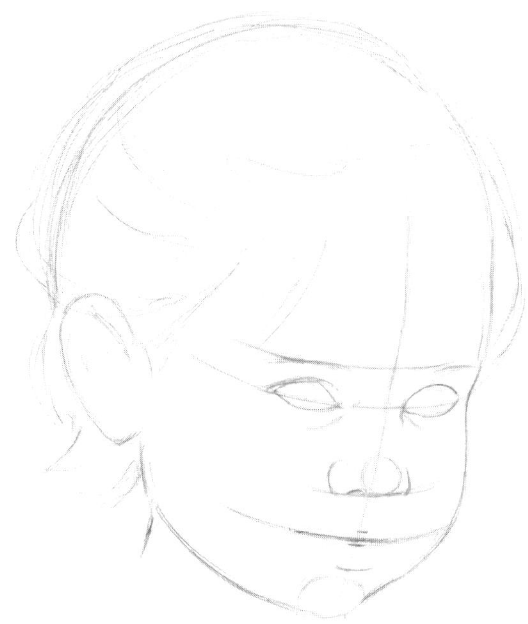

STEP 1   With a sharpened 2B pencil, I sketch the basic shape of the face. Using my knowledge of children's proportions as a guide, I lightly draw the guidelines, which curve slightly because of the viewpoint. I place the features below the horizontal centerline, where the eyebrows begin. I block in the round eyes, placing them a little more than one eye-width apart. Then I sketch the round nose and small mouth and add some wispy hair to frame the face.

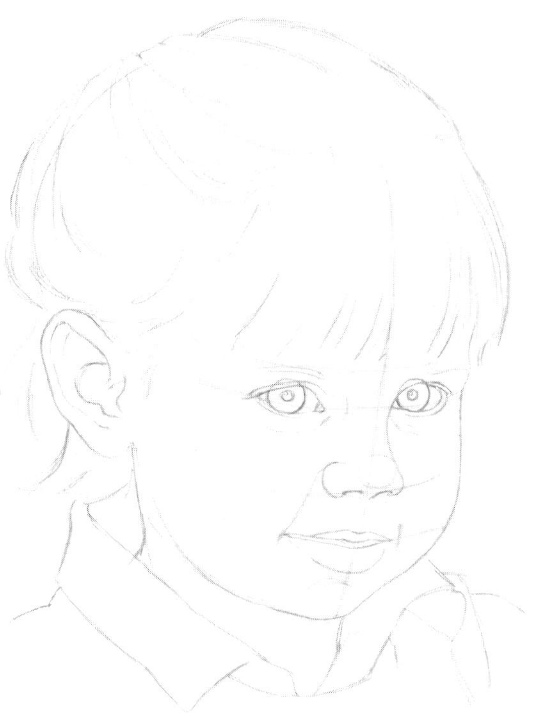

STEP 2   I add details to the eyes and indicate highlights. (Prominent highlights give children's eyes that curious, youthful spark.) Then I develop the ear and fill out the lips. I draw a curved line from the tip of the girl's left nostril up to her left eye to build up the nose and draw another line connecting the nose to the mouth, giving her right cheek form. I sketch a few quick lines to indicate the slightly chubby area underneath her eyes, extending the cheek a bit to round it out. I add the bangs with light, soft strokes.

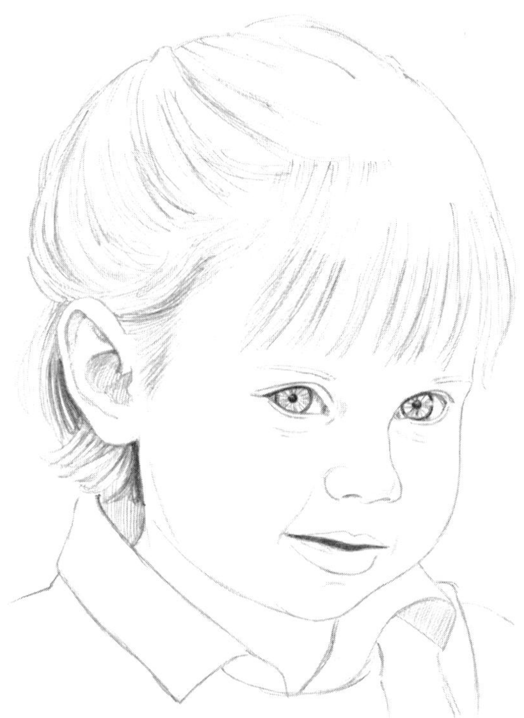

STEP 3   With a 3B pencil, I fill in the area between the lips, then shade the pupil and outline the iris. I add a few thin lines for hair between the scalp and the ear, darkening the hair where it is in shadow behind the ear. I keep the hair soft by sketching with light, short lines—this keeps my subject looking youthful. Switching back to the 2B pencil, I shade the inside of the ear and the underside of the shirt collar, helping to show the direction of the light source. Then I define the lines around the eyes and the mouth.

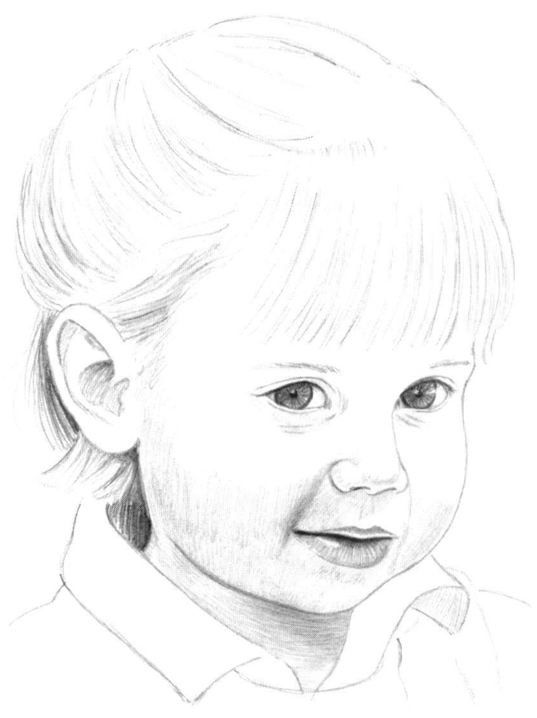

STEP 4   I shade the lips with a 2B pencil, leaving a light area on the bottom lip to give it shine. Then I shade the neck using light strokes that follow the shape of the neck. With a few short lines, I draw the eyebrows; I also add light shading to the lower half of the face, filling out the cheeks and making them look rosy.

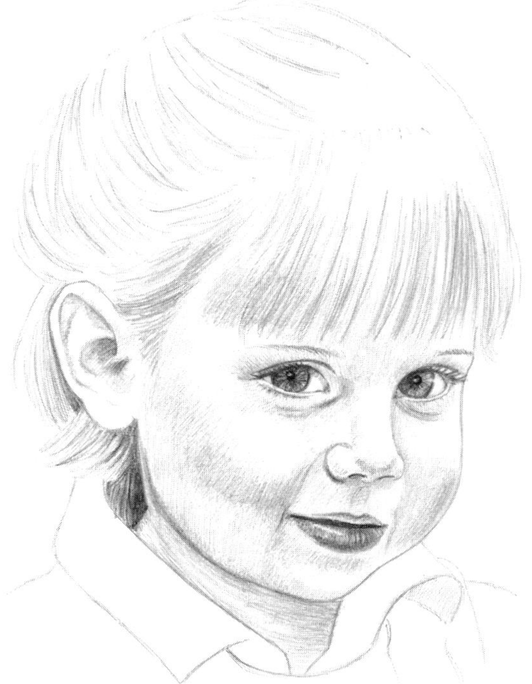

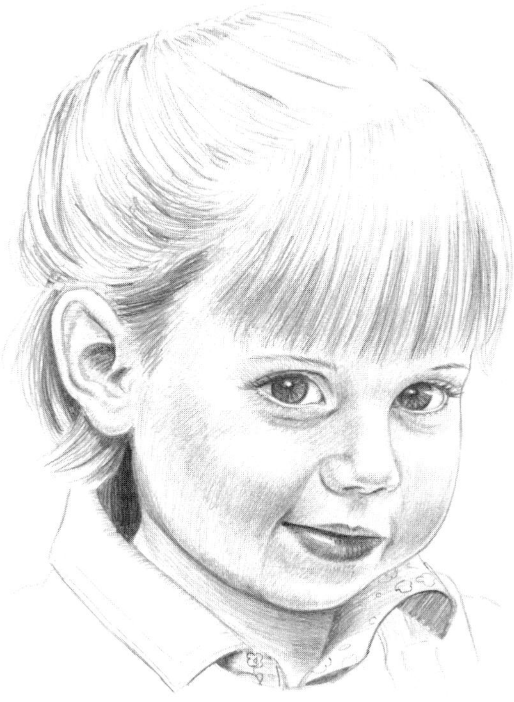

STEP 5 Over each eyelid, I sketch a series of small lines curving up to the eyebrows to show the youthful chubbiness. Then I add eyelashes using curved pencil strokes. To keep the subject looking young, I draw very light, almost nonexistent eyebrows. I shade the forehead in an up-and-down motion, and then I give her right cheek more form by darkening the areas around it. I use sweeping strokes to build up the bangs, leaving the paper white in areas for a shiny look.

STEP 6 Still using the 2B pencil, I further build up the ear. I shade a small area between the bottom of the nose and the top of the lips to suggest the indentation, and I add shading to the creases around the mouth. I create more dark strokes in the back of the hair to show where the hair is layered. Then I draw a flower pattern on the shirt collar. Adding youthful patterns to your subject's clothing helps define their age; overalls, jumpers, ribbons, baseball caps, and bows also can imply youth.

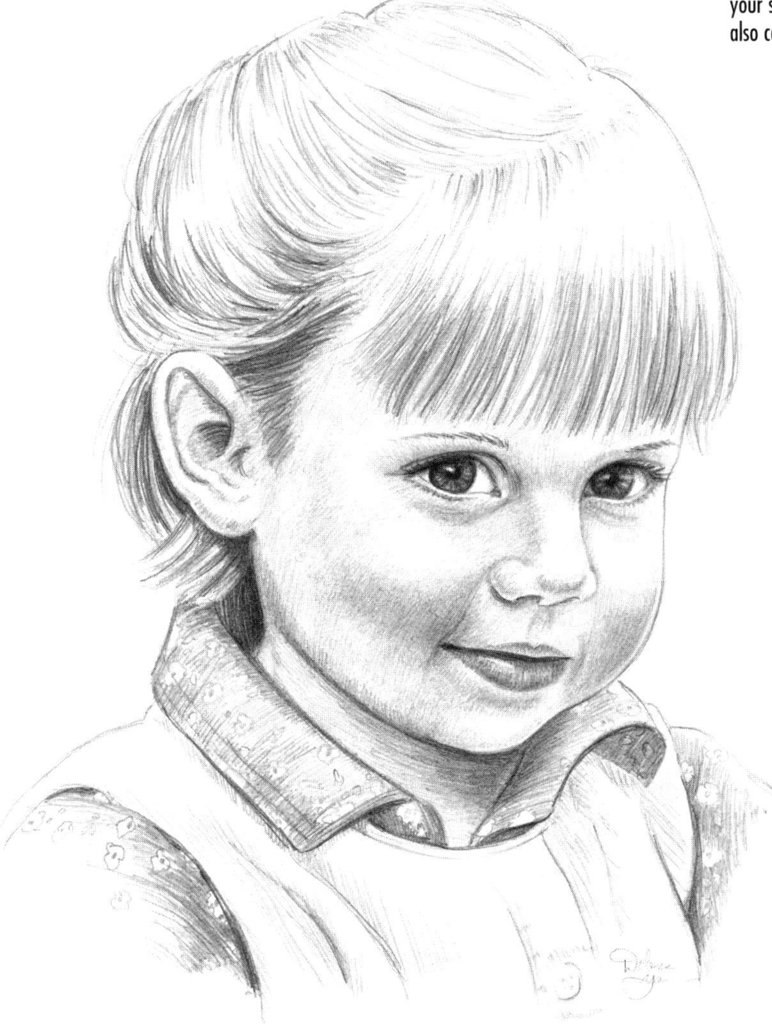

Drawing from a Different Angle

Because of the way this young girl's head is tilted back, you see more of her chin and neck than you do the top of her head. The ears appear a bit lower on the head, and you see more of the bottom parts of her eyes. You can even see the underside of the upper eyelid beneath the eyelashes. Even when drawing children from a different angle, the features remain rounded and childlike; for example, you can still get a sense of this girl's wide-eyed, curious expression, although you see less of the eyes than you would in a forward-facing view. And although the nostrils are a little more prominent in this view, they still retain their soft, smooth shape.

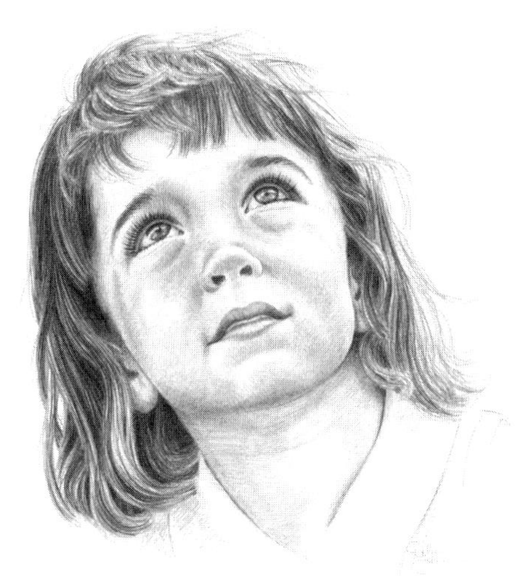

STEP 7 Putting my pencil aside for a moment, I carefully drag the edge of a kneaded eraser across the top of the bangs to create the appearance of blond hair. Using the 3B pencil, I create texture on the jumper and shirt by spacing the lines of the corduroy slightly apart from one another. Then I develop the floral pattern on the sleeves of her shirt. Finally I draw a small button, then stand back from my portrait and make sure the transitions from light to dark values are smooth and that there are no harsh or angular lines that might make the subject appear older than she is.

Rendering a Baby

Drawing babies can be tricky because it's easy to unintentionally make them look older than they are. The face gets longer in proportion to the cranium with age, so the younger the child, the lower the eyes are on the face (and thus, the larger the forehead). In addition, babies' eyes are disproportionately large in comparison to the rest of their bodies—so draw them this way!

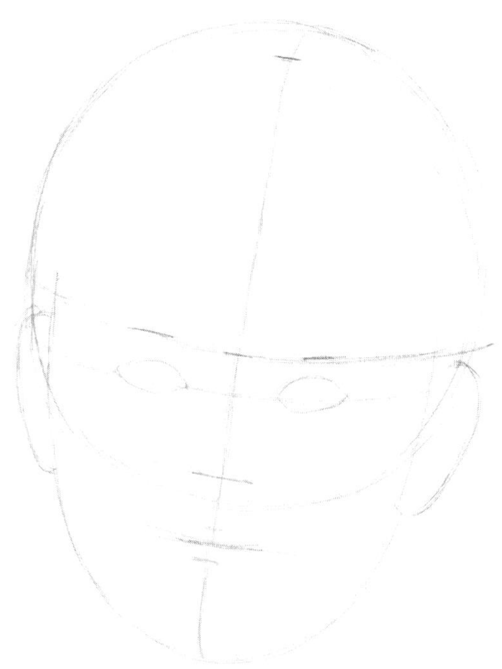

STEP 1   Using an HB pencil, I block in the cranial mass and the facial guidelines. (See page 20 for more information on placing a baby's features.) The head is tilted downward and turned slightly to its left, so I adjust the guidelines accordingly. I place the eyebrows at the horizontal centerline and the eyes in the lower half of the face.

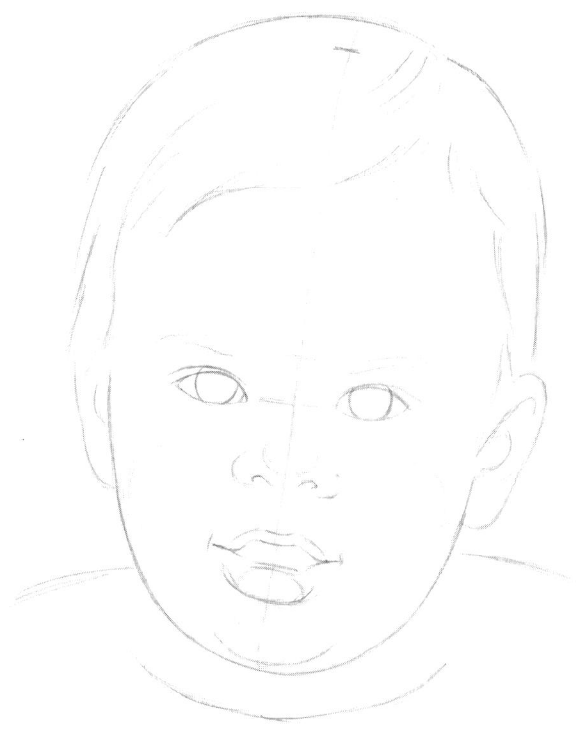

STEP 2   Now I create the fine hair using soft, short strokes and a B pencil. I draw the open mouth with the bottom lip resting against the chin. Then I add large irises that take up most of the eyes and suggest the small nose. I draw a curved line under the chin to suggest chubbiness; then I indicate the shoulders, omitting the neck.

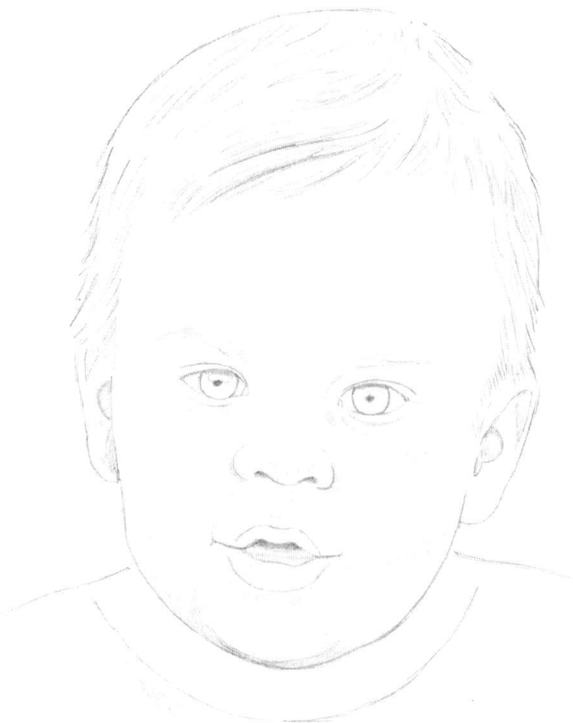

STEP 3   Erasing guidelines as I draw, I add pupils and highlights to the eyes with a B pencil. I lightly sketch more of the hair and eyebrows, then shade under the chin to give it form. I also shade inside the ears. Then I connect and refine the lips, shading the upturned corners to suggest the pudgy mouth. I shade the inside of the mouth, showing that there aren't any teeth; then I further define the neckline of the shirt.

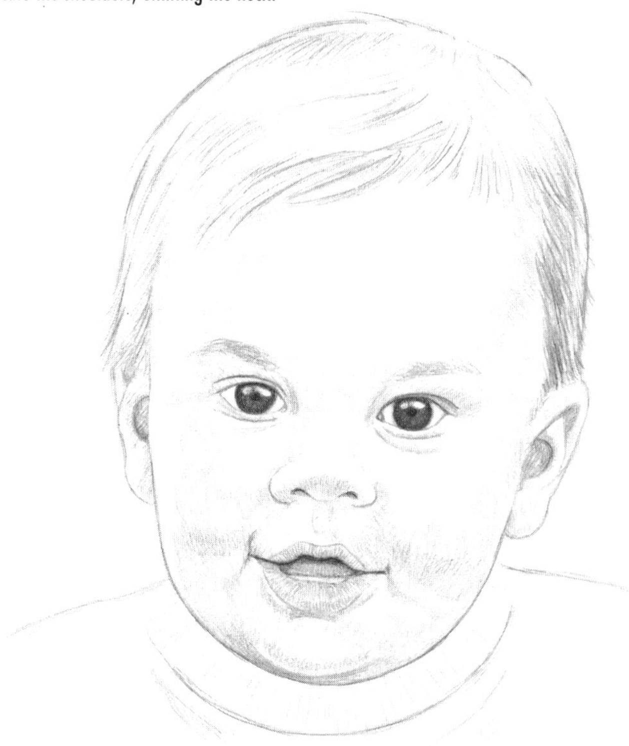

STEP 4   With a 2B pencil, I shade the irises, and then go back in and lighten the highlights with a kneaded eraser. I draw more soft strokes in the hair and eyebrows and shade the lips and face. I emphasize the pudgy mouth by softly shading the smile lines, then finally add curving lines to the neckline of the shirt.

STEP 5 I continue
shading the face, then
add another light layer of
shading to the lips. I use the
end of a kneaded eraser to
pull out a highlight on the
bottom lip. Then I draw
some very light eyelashes.
I create darker values in the
hair and eyebrows and round
out the outline of the face.
I also lightly shade the shirt.
Then I take a step back from
the portrait to assess whether
I've properly built up the
roundness in the cheeks,
chin, eyes, nose, and mouth.
I use a blending stump to
gently blend transitions in my
shading to make the com-
plexion baby smooth.

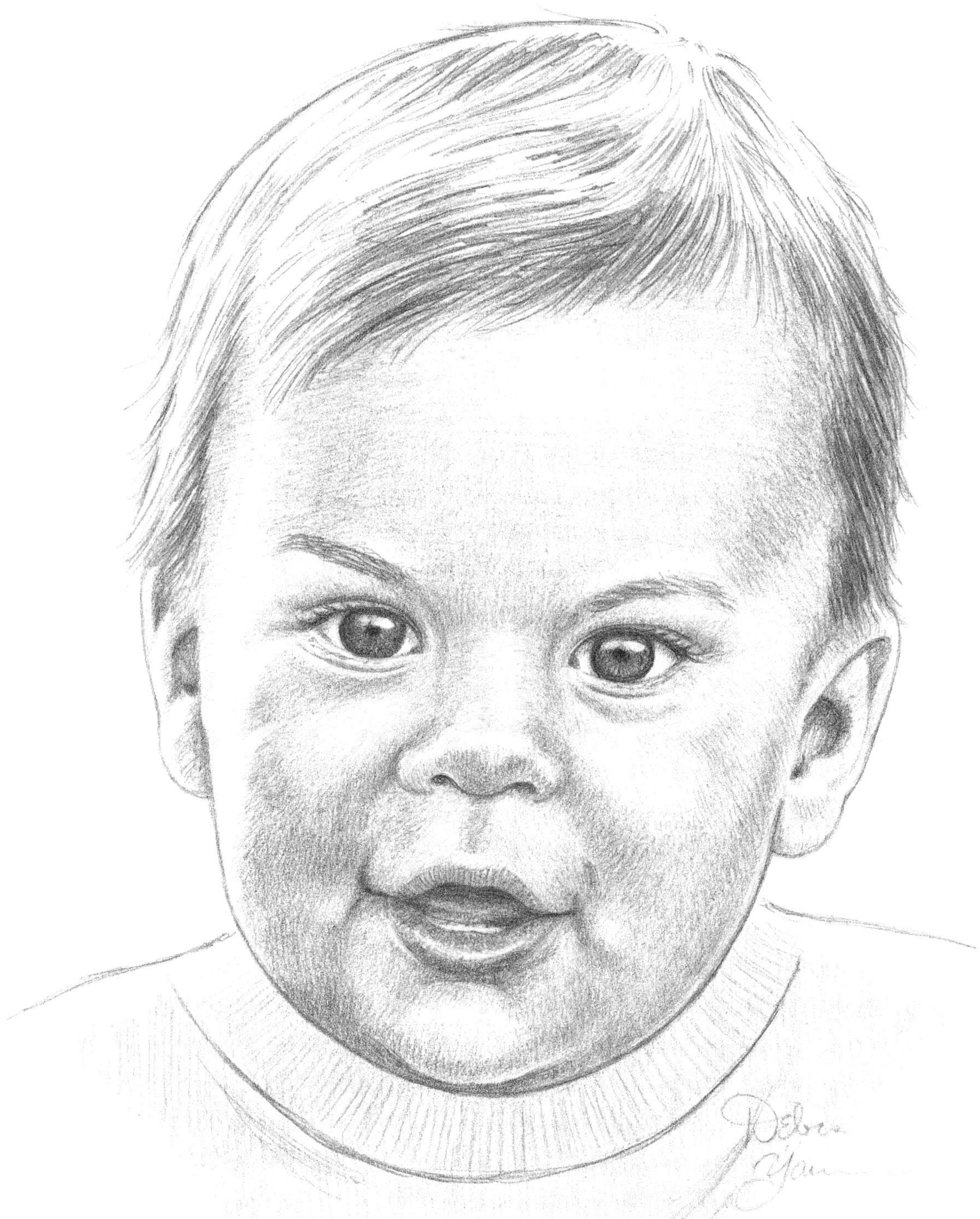

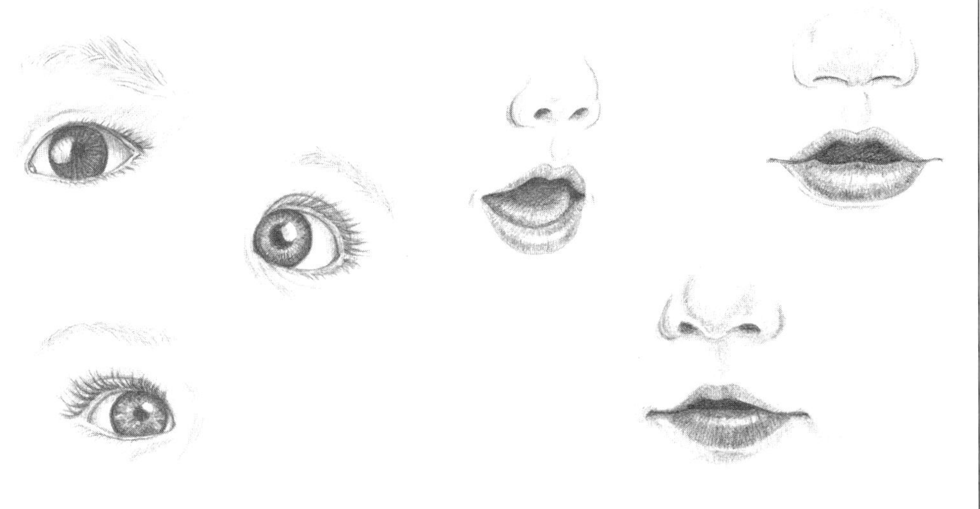

Drawing a Baby's Features

Babies often have wide-eyed, curious expres-sions. Try curving the eyebrows upward to create the appearance of childlike curiosity; pull out highlights in each eye to add life and interest to your drawing. A baby's lips have a soft, pudgy appearance, and the mouth is usually not as wide as an adult's is. Adding highlights is important to convey a smooth texture, and creating creases at the corners of the mouth will help indicate youthful chubbiness.

Choosing a Photo Reference

If you're using a photograph as a reference while you draw, it's usually best to have several different photographs from varying angles and with different light sources to choose from. Not only does this give you a wider selection of poses and lighting options, but it also allows you to combine different elements from each photograph. For example, if you are satisfied with the lighting in one photograph but you're drawn to the facial expression in another, you can combine the best parts from each for your portrait.

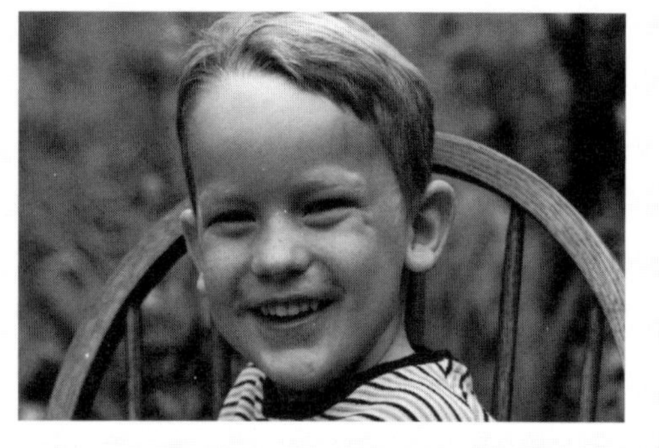

A

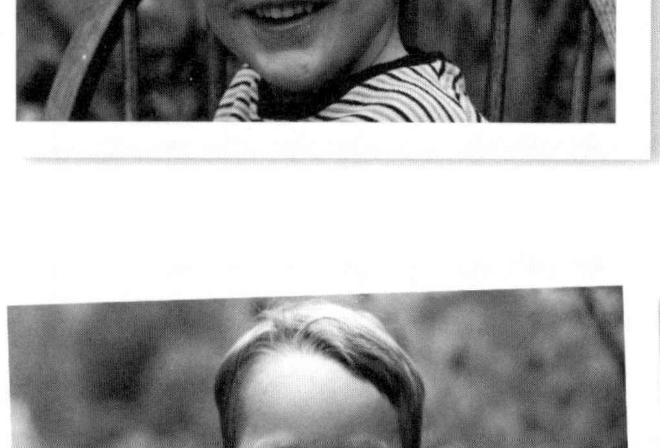

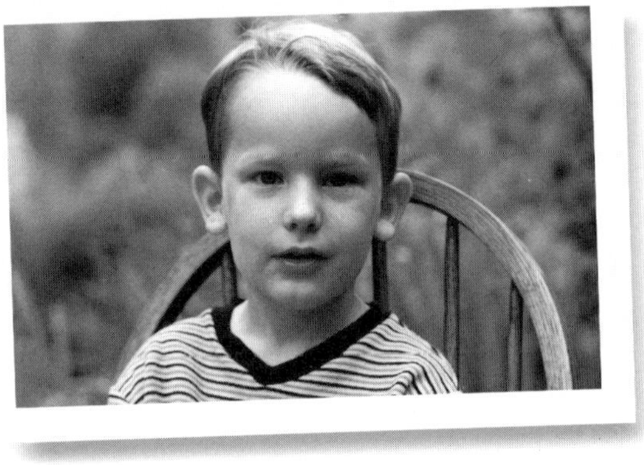

B

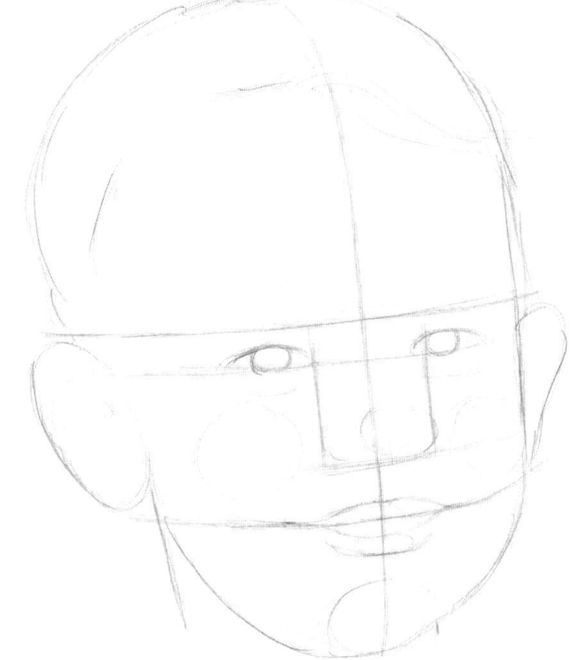

STEP 1 After studying my selection of photographs I choose the best one and use it as a reference to block in the outline of the face, the guidelines, and the features.

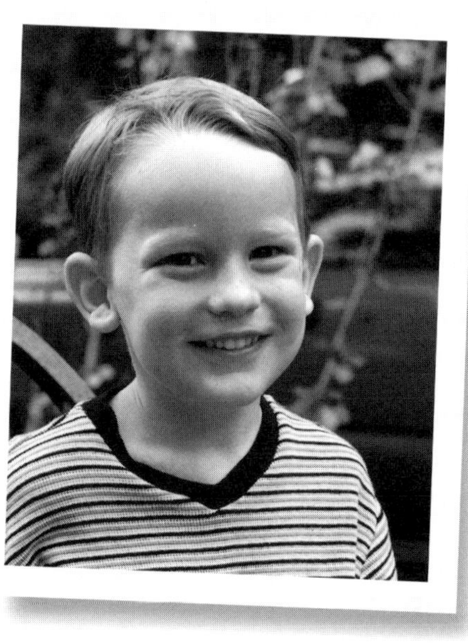

C

FINDING THE BEST POSE In photo A, the subject's eyes are squinting just a tad too much. In photo B, the subject's pose seems stiff and stilted. But in photo C, his pose and expression are just right!

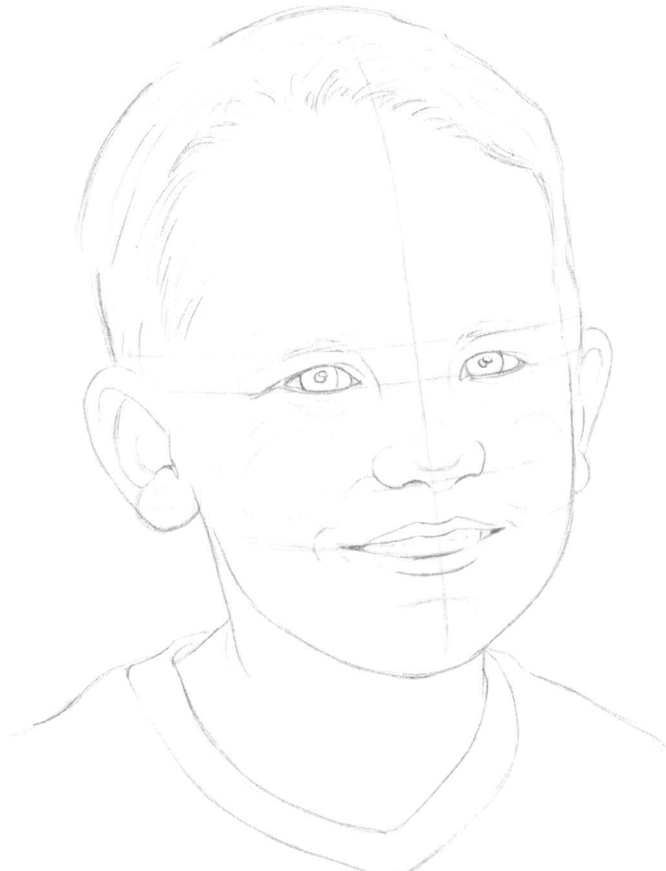

STEP 2 I compare my initial sketch with the photograph and make necessary adjustments, indicating the roundness of the bottoms of the earlobes with light circles. Next I draw the slightly protruding teeth.

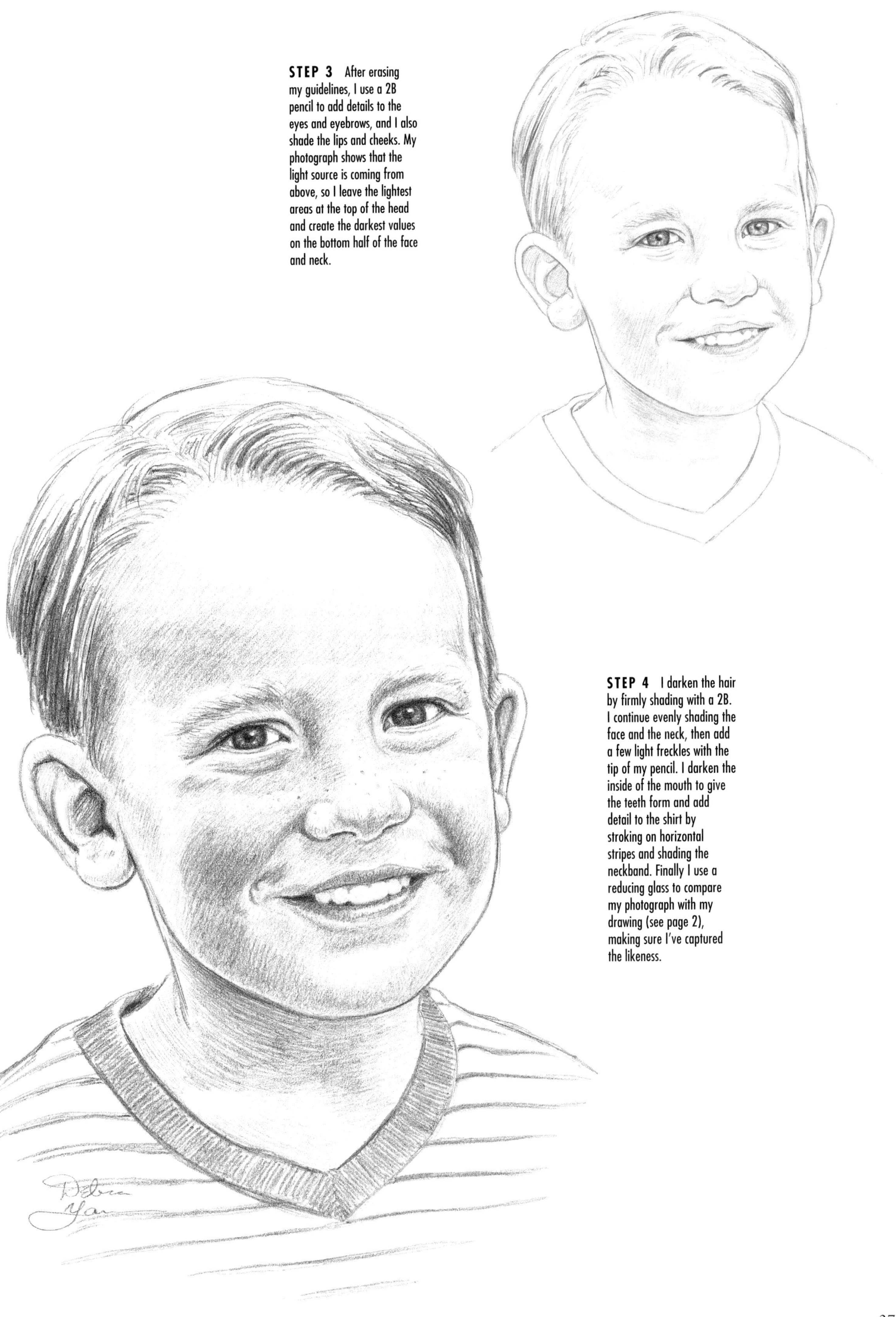

STEP 3 After erasing my guidelines, I use a 2B pencil to add details to the eyes and eyebrows, and I also shade the lips and cheeks. My photograph shows that the light source is coming from above, so I leave the lightest areas at the top of the head and create the darkest values on the bottom half of the face and neck.

STEP 4 I darken the hair by firmly shading with a 2B. I continue evenly shading the face and the neck, then add a few light freckles with the tip of my pencil. I darken the inside of the mouth to give the teeth form and add detail to the shirt by stroking on horizontal stripes and shading the neckband. Finally I use a reducing glass to compare my photograph with my drawing (see page 2), making sure I've captured the likeness.

Indicating Fair Features

When drawing a subject with fair skin and hair, keep your shading to a minimum; apply just enough medium and dark values to create the illusion of form without creating the appearance of color. Draw blond hair by outlining the general shape, then adding a few carefully placed strokes to suggest the hair style and create some dimension. Keep in mind that light, wispy eyebrows and freckles often accompany fair skin and hair.

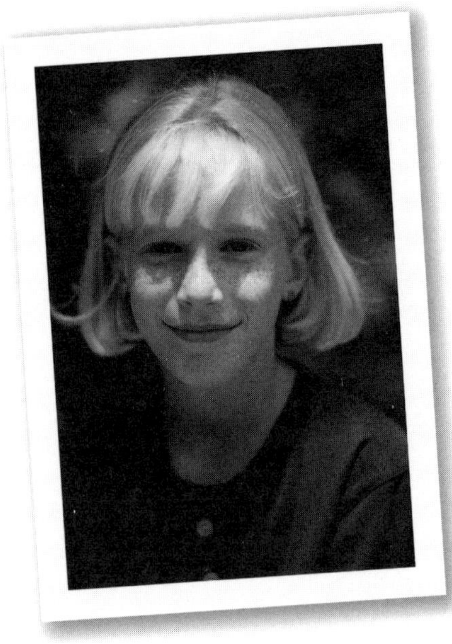

SHADING FAIR SKIN AND HAIR In this photo, the overhead light makes the bangs, nose, and cheeks look nearly pure white, so I avoid these areas when shading my drawing, leaving much of the paper white.

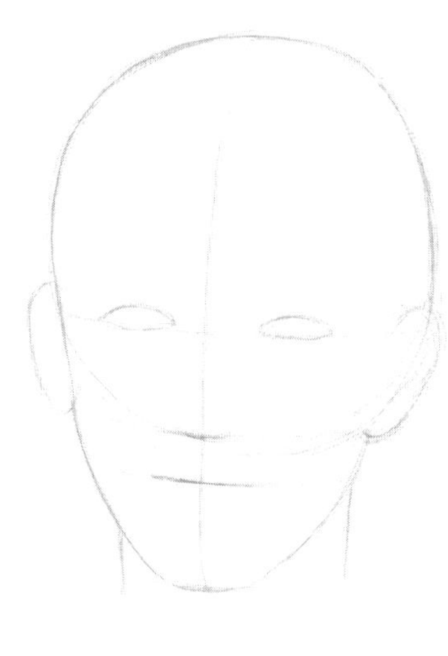

STEP 1 First I lay out the face with an HB pencil. The face is slightly tilted to the subject's left, so I shift the vertical centerline to the left a bit as well. I lightly place the eyes, nose, mouth, and ears, then block in her long, slender neck.

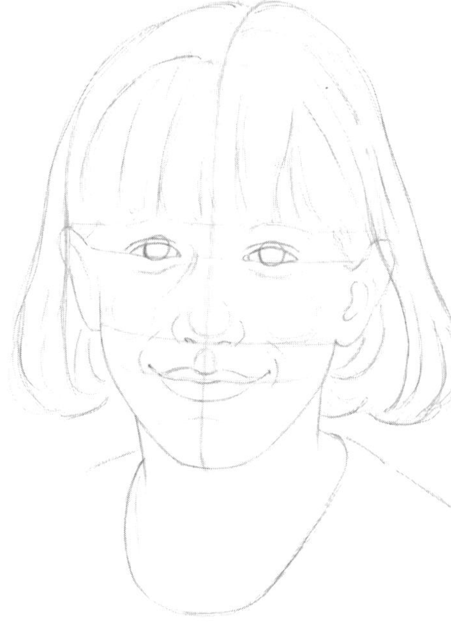

STEP 2 Switching to a 2B pencil, I develop the features. Although I use the photo for a reference, I use *artistic license* to adjust my rendering as I see fit. For example, I sketch the bangs so they fall straight onto her forehead, rather than being swept to the side as they are in the photo. I also omit the strand of hair that is blowing in the wind.

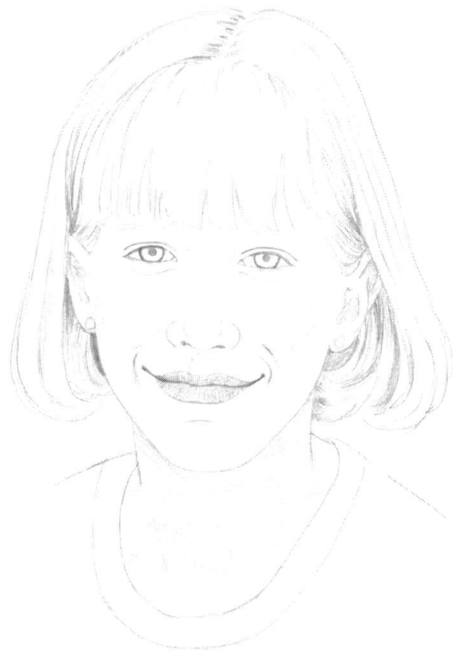

STEP 3 Now I refine the features, erasing my guidelines as I draw. I continue building up the hair, leaving the top and sides mostly white, adding only a few dark strands here and there. The darkest values are around the ears where the hair is in shadow. Next I add small circles for the earrings and shade the insides of the ears. I develop the lips, then use horizontal strokes to shade the neck.

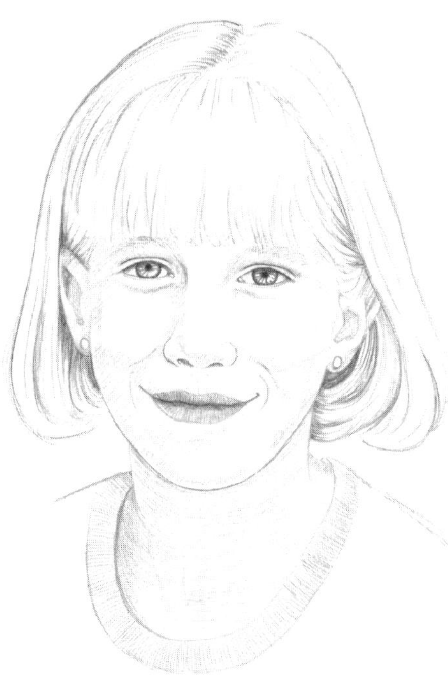

STEP 4 I shade the face with light, soft strokes to depict the subject's fair skin. Then I make short, quick strokes for the eyebrows, keeping them light and soft to indicate blond hair. Next I shade the irises using strokes that radiate out from the pupil. I also add some hatching strokes to the neckband of the shirt.

Depicting Fine Hair

Blond hair is often finer than darker hair, especially in children. Draw fine hair in narrow sections, leaving plenty of white areas showing through the dark values. Add some short, wispy strands of hair at the forehead to frame the face.

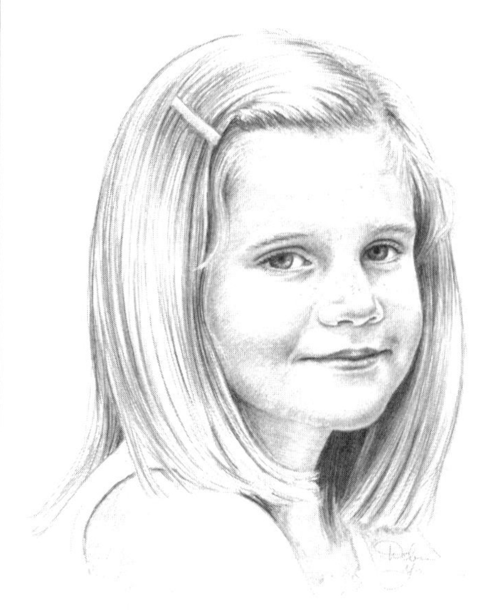

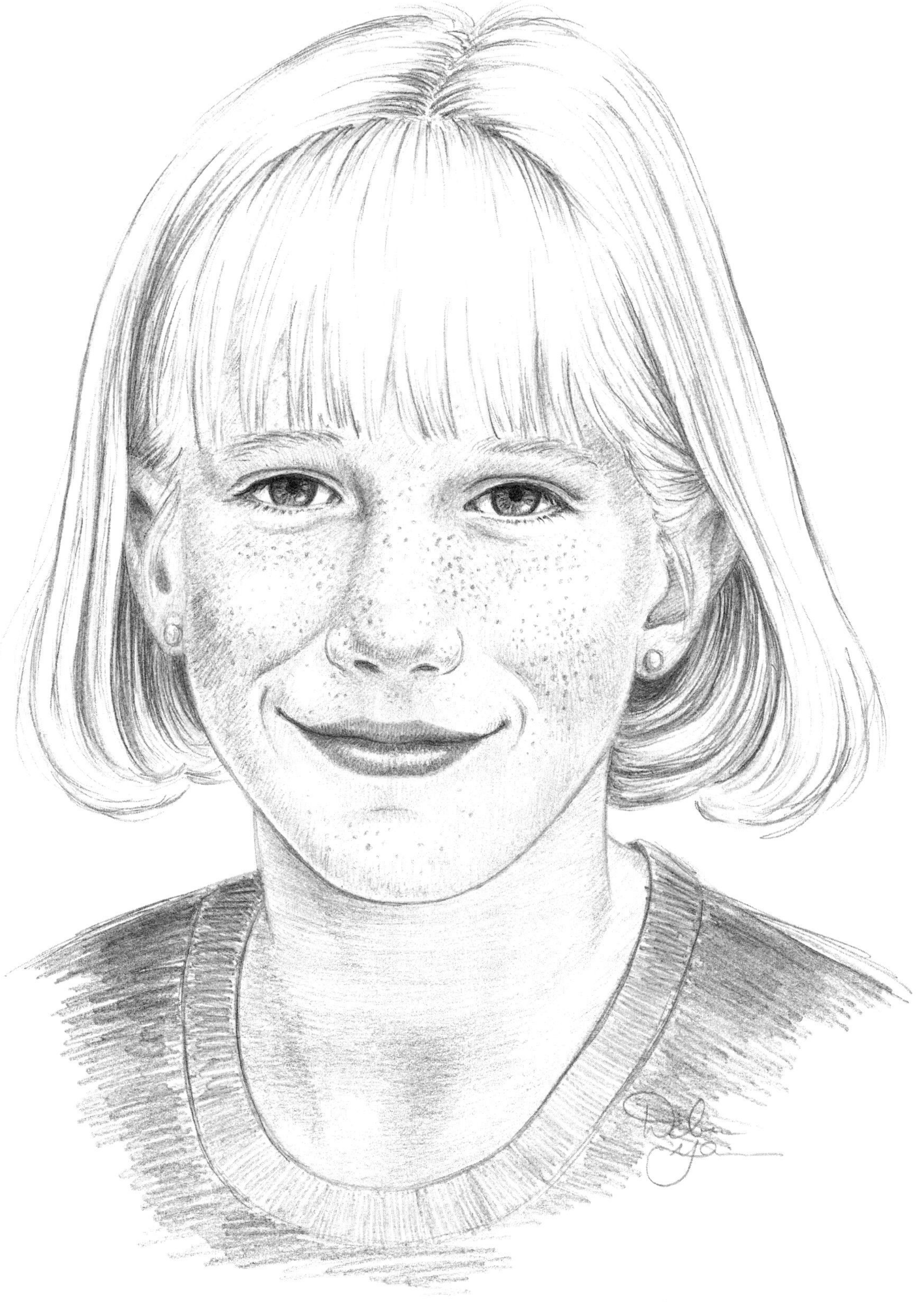

Finally I shade the shirt, using relatively dark strokes. It's easy for a blond subject to look washed out on white paper, so the dark values in the shirt help frame the subject and make her face stand out.

Creating Realistic Freckles

To draw freckles, space them sporadically, in varying sizes and distances from one other. You don't have to replicate every freckle on your subject's face—just draw the general shapes and let the viewer's eye fill in the rest.

▶ **WHAT TO DO**   Make sure some of the freckles overlap, and make some light and some dark by varying the pressure you place on the pencil.

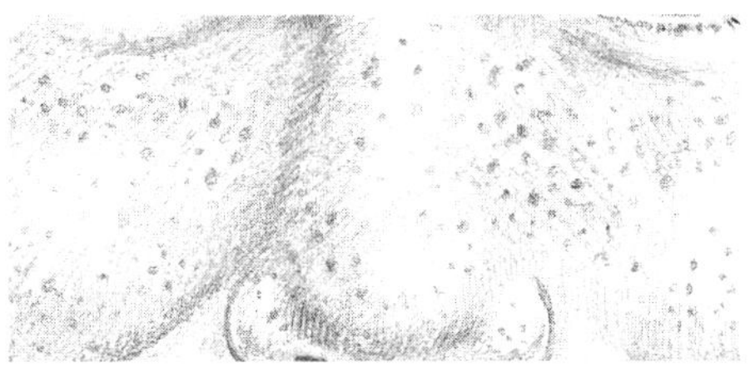

▶ **WHAT NOT TO DO**
When drawing freckles, do not space them too evenly or make them equal in size, as shown here. These freckles look more like polka dots!

Replicating Dark Skin Tones

When depicting dark skin tones, pay attention to the value of the skin tone and how it compares with the values of the features; for example, when the skin is dark, the lips need to be shaded even more heavily. In addition, look for differences in features that indicate ethnicity or race, such as the nose, lips, or eye shapes and the hair color or texture.

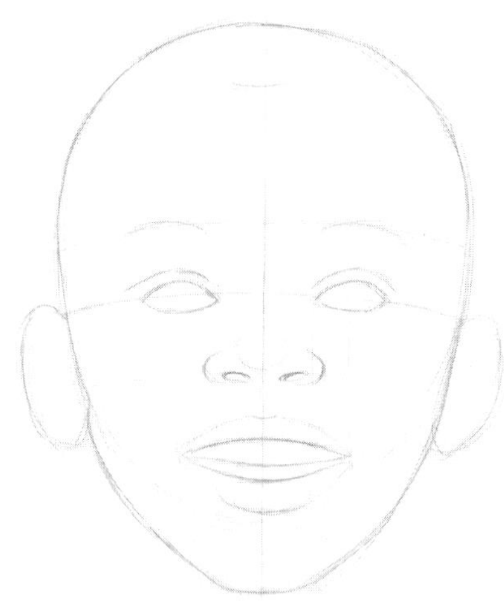

STEP 1   With a 2B pencil, I block in the basic head shape and place the features, following the guidelines. I draw the almond-shaped eyes, wide nose, and full lips, accurately depicting the features as I see them. Then I block in the teeth and indicate the hairline, eyebrows, and ears.

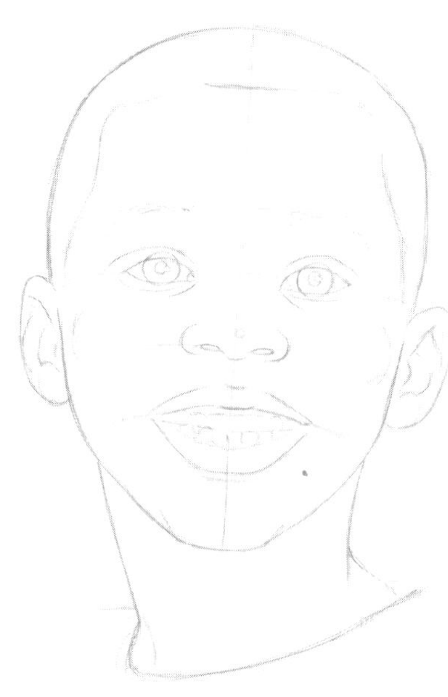

STEP 2   Still using the 2B pencil, I sketch in the curved neck and define the chin. Then I develop the eyes and use short, quick lines to draw the eyebrows. Next I start defining the ears and teeth. Then I block in the hairline and the neckline of the shirt.

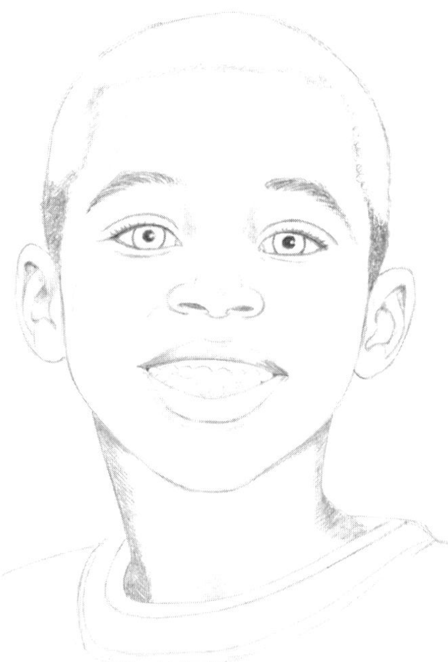

STEP 3   Next I shade the nose, neck, and top lip, trying to make the lip appear full. I shade the nostrils relatively dark so they will stand out against the dark skin. Using quick, circul strokes, I start to render the short, curly hair. Then I detail the eyebrows and eyes and define the neckband of the shirt.

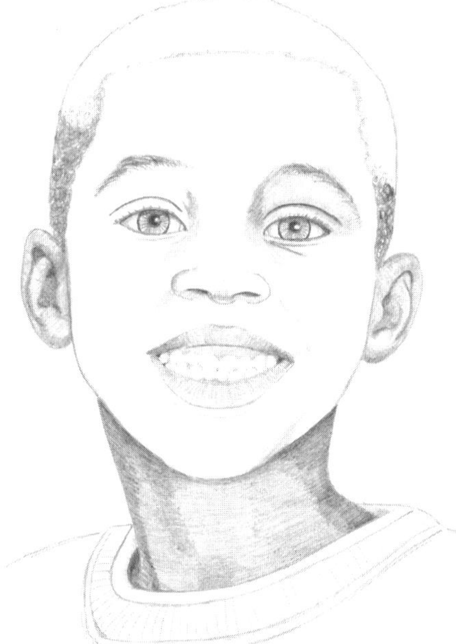

STEP 4   Using strokes that follow the shape of the mouth, I continue shading the lips; then I shade the gums, carefully working around the teeth. I make sure the lips and gums won't contrast too sharply with the skin, because if they're too dark they'll look unnatural. Next I build up the coarse hair with more circular strokes. Then I move to the neck, using horizontal lines that curve with the shape of the neck. Notice how these lines overlap and blend into the shading that was applied in step 3.

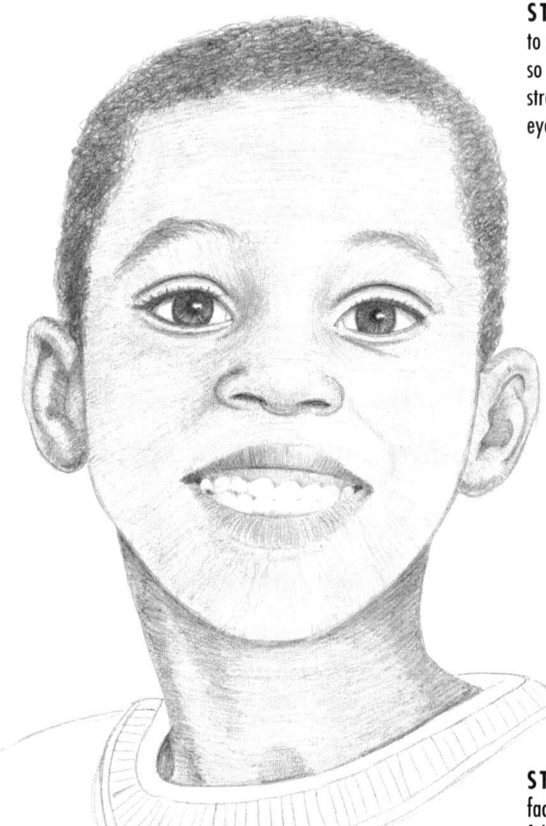

STEP 5   Now I apply a light layer of shading over the enti face, always varying the direction of my strokes as necessary follow the shapes of the different planes. The shading is starti to round out the face, which has looked a bit flat up to this point. I'll add more shading later to make it appear even rounder and fuller.

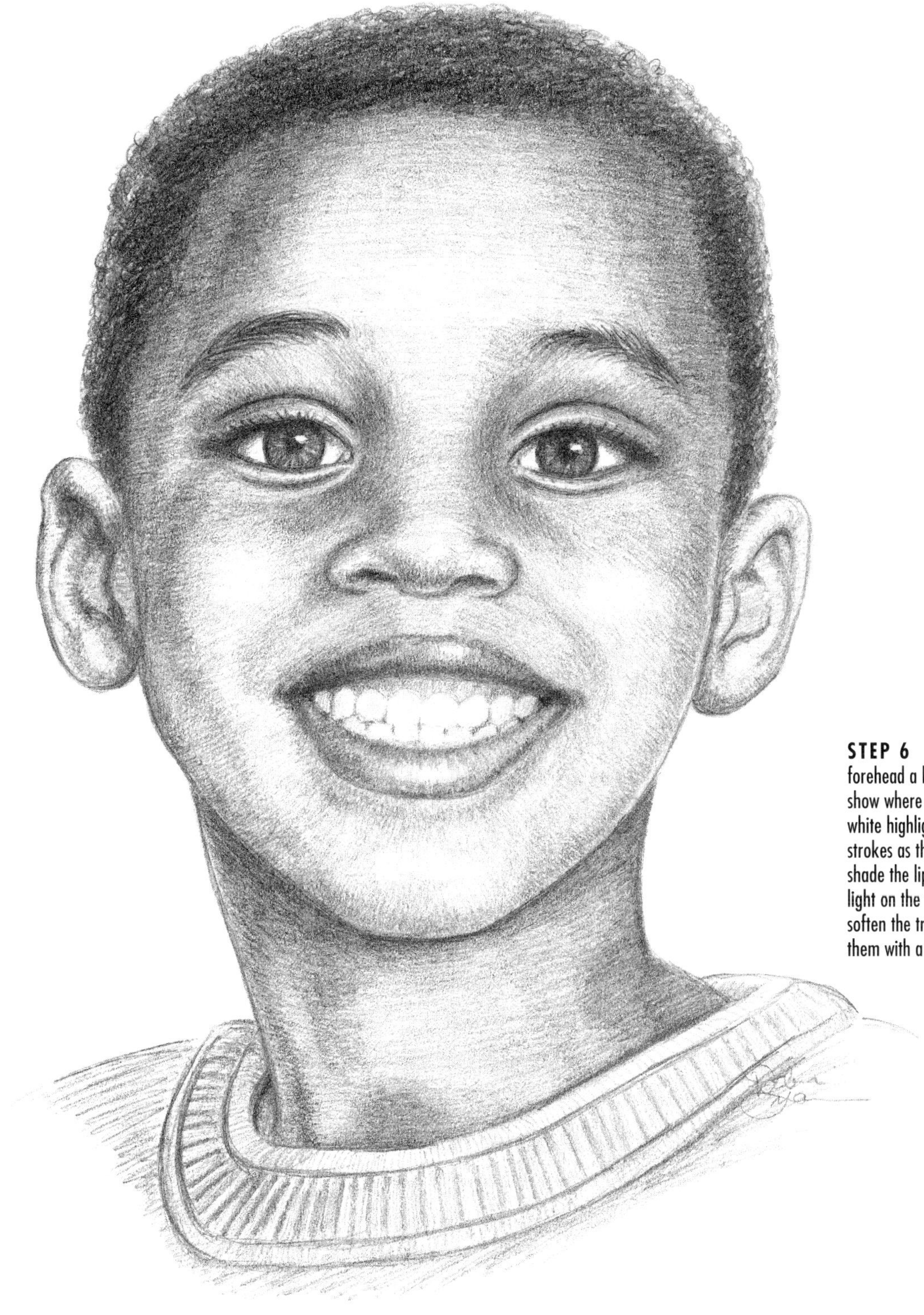

Establishing Values

Every skin tone is made up of a variety of values—when drawing in graphite pencil, you can accurately capture these differing tones using varying degrees of light and shadow. Before you start drawing, be sure to study your subject to establish the richest darks and brightest lights of their skin tone, whether they are fair-, medium-, or dark-skinned. In the examples at right, hair color and contrasting values work together to suggest the medium skin tone of the boy to the far left and the fair skin tone of the boy at center. The darkly shaded, fully formed cheeks of the boy to the far right give his skin a ruddy, tanned appearance.

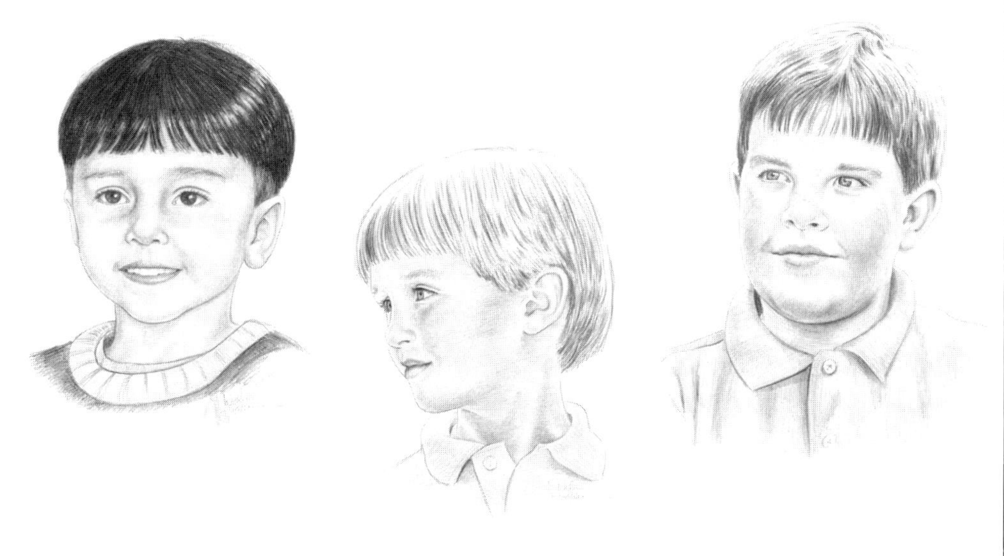